Theory and Practice of the Balance of Power

1486–1914

SELECTED EUROPEAN WRITINGS

Edited by Moorhead Wright
Department of International Politics
University College of Wales, Aberystwyth

Dent, London
Rowman and Littlefield, Totowa, N.J.

51160

© J. M. Dent & Sons Ltd, 1975
All rights reserved
Made in Great Britain
at the
Aldine Press · Letchworth · Herts
for
J. M. DENT & SONS LTD
Aldine House · 26 Albemarle Street · London
First published 1975
First published in the United States 1975
by ROWMAN AND LITTLEFIELD, Totowa, N.J.

Dent edition
ISBN 0 460 10196 x

Rowman and Littlefield edition
ISBN 0-87471-407-9

Contents

Preface

Of the ideas associated with the development of the European state-system none has been the subject of more speculation and analysis than the balance of power. There are thus considerable difficulties in selecting a representative anthology of the rich literature, spanning more than four centuries.

My primary aim has been to trace the evolution of the idea of the balance of power from the simple description of balanced antagonisms in the Italian Renaissance to the concept of a complex and delicate mechanism for the maintenance of a system of independent states in modern Europe. This objective has led me to emphasize abstract and speculative writing which shows an awareness of an evolving tradition of thought and debate. Against these I have set a number of state papers as well as selections from notable statesmen-historians such as Guicciardini, Bolingbroke and Churchill.

I have tried to give the sixteenth and seventeenth centuries a fairly ample quota, for the writings of this formative period are less well known than those of the eighteenth century onwards. There are fewer selections from the late nineteenth century since the elaboration of the idea, if not its application, reached its high point in the period of the Napoleonic Wars and their aftermath. In order to make room for some unfamiliar writings I have regretfully had to sacrifice some well-known ones. These are, however, noticed in the bibliography.

My earlier researches on the balance of power have benefited from discussions with Professor Robert E. Osgood and Dr William C. Olson. I am grateful to my colleagues Mr Keith Hamilton, who pointed out the speech by Sir Edward Grey, and shared his extensive knowledge of the diplomacy of this era, and Dr Brian Porter, who helpfully commented upon a draft of the introduction. My thanks also go to Dr Barbara Haines, Dr Patricia M. Sherwood and Mr John Warrington for their specially commissioned translations; and to Mrs Gwalia Watkins and Mrs Kay Critchley for typing the manuscript. My greatest debt is to my wife, whose encouragement and help at every stage made such a difference.

Aberystwyth, 1974   MOORHEAD WRIGHT

Acknowledgments

Extract from *The History of Italy* (p. 7) reprinted by permission of Macmillan Publishing Co., Inc. Copyright © 1969 Sidney Alexander.

Extract on p. 134 reprinted from *The World Crisis 1911–14* by Winston Churchill, by permission of
The Hamlyn Publishing Group Limited, and of
Charles Scribner's Sons. Copyright 1923 Charles Scribner's Sons.

TEXTS AND TRANSLATIONS

The translations used in this book derive from a variety of sources, some contemporary with their originals, some of more recent date. Those selections not specially translated for the present edition, as well as passages by English writers, are reproduced from the sources to which they are attributed, except for some modernization of older spelling and typographic devices, and correction of errors and omissions.

Introduction

The quest for origins is a notoriously difficult task, and the difficulty is all the greater when the subject is such an ambiguous compound of abstract speculation and historical practice as the balance of power. Historians have generally traced the origins of the balance of power to the Italian Renaissance; they have tended to interpret the second half of the fifteenth century in Italy in terms of a relatively self-contained system composed of five major city-states who sought to prevent the domination of the peninsula by any one power.[1] This system is said to have lasted from the Peace of Lodi (1454), which ended the long series of struggles against Milanese domination, to the descent of Charles VIII of France into Italy, initiating the Italian wars of the sixteenth century. To a considerable extent the historiographical tradition can be traced back to Guicciardini's portrayal of this 'golden age' in the opening pages of his *History of Italy*, which are reprinted here (pp. 7–12). Recently, however, it has been coming under closer scrutiny. Giovanni Pillinini, most notably, has explored the political and historiographical myths arising from the period and set against them the historical record.[2] The main counter-arguments against the accepted version are these: the system was not as self-contained and isolated from foreign intervention before 1494 as has been maintained; there was considerable inequality in strength and position among even the five greater Italian powers; and the assignment of the role of the Italian league (formed in 1455 by Milan, Florence, Venice, Rome and Naples) in the balance of power is misconceived.

The central figure in the traditional interpretation is of course Lorenzo de' Medici, whose reputation as *l'ago della bilancia* ('the tongue of the balance') is most directly responsible for the attribution of balance-of-power politics to this period. Modern Italian scholarship on Lorenzo's statecraft has been heavily under the influence of this tradition and has in turn influenced general histories of the Italian Renaissance.[3] Until we have a full-length 'revisionist' study of Lorenzo's diplomacy based on his correspondence, we will be unable to assess Lorenzo's true place in the balance-of-power tradition, but the two letters translated and printed in this anthology (pp. 1–7) suggest that his diplomacy was not guided by a consistent, reasoned principle of balanced power as a state of affairs to be

brought about in Italy as a whole. Lorenzo's scepticism about the
value of foreign intervention can only by implication be associated
with the idea of a balance of power in Italy; with hindsight, of
course, we see that it was the lack of caution in this respect which
precipitated and prolonged the turbulent Italian wars which lasted
from 1494 to 1559. Indeed it became one of the main rules of 'Machiavellian' diplomacy to get the better of your neighbour by calling in
foreign aid. In contrast we find Paolo Paruta, in the extract from his
Political Discourses (pp. 15–19), looking back after a century of bitter
experience and reflecting on the circumstances, in terms of the balance
of power, in which it was wise to avoid foreign intervention.

Despite the qualifications which ought to be made to the widely
accepted version of the origins of the balance of power, we should
not underestimate the general influence of this period on the subsequent development of the idea. It was, as Pillinini aptly puts it,
'*un equilibrio di egoismi*' in which the egoism of one state was balanced
or offset by the egoism of another.[4] This provided a rudimentary and
precarious basis for order. It was indeed the logical and historical
precursor of the more highly developed notion of the balance of
power as an expression of 'ethical-cultural unity' which became the
basis of later conceptions of a European comity of nation-states.[5]
Envy and fear inspired this equilibrium in a world characterized by
'the neighbourhood of a large number of states, too unequal to
escape mutual fear, but equal enough to resist one another'.[6] The
same conditions were soon to prevail in early modern Europe. The
main precepts of this purely self-regarding notion of the balance of
power were well summarized by Johann Gottlieb Fichte in 1804–5:

> What we ourselves cannot acquire, no other shall acquire, because
> his power would thereby obtain a disproportionate addition.

> If we cannot hinder others from aggrandizing themselves, then
> we must also secure for ourselves a proportionate aggrandizement.[7]

It was in fact a fairly simple idea of proportion or equality which
characterized the earliest foreshadowings of the new principle. In
the second half of the fifteenth century, Vespasiano da Bisticci, in his
Lives of Famous Men, praised the foreign policy of Cosimo de' Medici in
terms suggestive of the new idea. Vespasiano reports that Cosimo was
always afraid of the consequences if Venice became so powerful that
Florence would be endangered, and so did everything to decrease the
Venetians' power. The period of peace which Florence enjoyed in the
middle of the fifteenth century was credited by Vespasiano to Cosimo's
ability to 'reduce the powers of Italy to that equality to which he

brought them, and particularly the Venetians'.[8] In many early allusions to balance, particularly the *elogia* of Lorenzo de' Medici, the metaphor is rather generally or loosely intended. In the widely cited *De Bello Italico* of Bernardo Rucellai it is 'the affairs of Italy' which 'hung in equal balance'.[9] And in Guicciardini's famous account of Lorenzo's policy it was 'the Italian situation' which was kept in balance. But Guicciardini greatly enriched the vocabulary of equilibrium by introducing terms such as 'counterpoise' and the implied notion of scales 'which did not incline to one side or the other'. More importantly, Guicciardini reveals an increasing sophistication in the analysis of power relations and their consequences. For example, he compares the power of Venice with that of the coalition (Naples, Milan, Florence and lesser states) formed in 1480: 'The principal aim of the pact was to prevent the Venetians from becoming any more powerful since they were undoubtedly stronger than any of the allies alone, but much weaker than all of them together.' Although this coalition restrained Venetian cupidity, their own envy and jealousy divided them more than the anti-Venetian cause united them. The three main features of the balance-of-power system are contained *in nuce* in this passage, namely, continuous vigilance and observation of each other; prevention of any increase in territory or 'reputation'; stable peace as a consequence.

The appeal of the stronger side was considerable in an acquisitive milieu, but the maxim of 'divide and rule' could be turned into a defensive maxim as well as an offensive one. And advice on which side to join, while often equivocal, came more clearly to favour joining the weaker side to counterbalance the stronger one. Machiavelli's counsel against joining an aggressive alliance with someone more powerful than oneself was based on the likelihood of becoming the prisoner of one's ally, while Philippe de Béthune's justification for joining the weakest side was that one 'might balance the power of the strongest, and by this counterpoise reduce them to reason' (p. 34). Again, Paolo Paruta's criticism of Pope Leo X (pp. 15–19) is based on the 'general rule' that 'to join in friendship and confederacy with a more powerful Prince, and one who is a near neighbour, when an increase of its power is intended by this conjunction, is never to be done without danger, nor ought such a resolution ever to be taken but out of great necessity'. On the contrary, Leo 'ought chiefly to have endeavoured in this conjuncture of affairs to have kept these scales even by his neutrality'.

It is noteworthy that Paruta assumed Leo's motives were based on the 'good of Italy' in that he sought to free Italy from 'the subjection of foreigners'. Paruta's framework of analysis is Italy as a whole rather than individual entities such as the Papal States and Venice. Paruta undoubtedly idealized the true state of affairs, particularly with regard to Venice, whose policies in the sixteenth century he often sought to justify in his writings. But it nonetheless represents a significant shift of orientation from the earlier sixteenth-century writings. Guicciardini, for example, correctly attributed Lorenzo's concern for 'Italian affairs' to the latter's realization that 'it would be most perilous to the Florentine Republic and to himself if any of the major powers should extend their area of dominion' (p. 9). Shortly after Paruta's *Political Discourses* the distinction was made explicit for the first time in Giovanni Botero's essay on the counterpoise of princes' forces, the first English translation of which appears in this volume (pp. 19–23). Botero distinguishes two kinds of purpose served by the art of counterpoise: 'For sometimes its purpose is the peace of a republic consisting of many different states, such as Italy, Germany, and Christendom as a whole, and at the other times the security and well-being of one particular state.' That Botero viewed these two kinds of counterpoise as mutually exclusive is suggested by the fact that the latter includes expansion, which would be contrary to the proportion required for the former.

This duality is a recurrent one in the history of the idea of the balance of power. Henry Kissinger, for example, has distinguished between a general equilibrium 'which makes it risky for one power or group of powers to attempt to impose its will on the remainder' and a special equilibrium 'which defines the historical relation of certain powers among each other'. The former is 'a mechanical expression of the balance of forces', the latter 'a reconciliation of historical aspirations'.[10] This formulation would seem to offer no prospects of *theoretical* reconciliation, despite the obvious practical necessity of doing so. Yet it is possible to argue that many of the theoretical expositions of the balance of power since Botero's essay have been devoted to reconciling the two imperatives of self-interest and common interest.

The surest link was necessity. *Communis necessitas facit communes amicos* was invoked about 1600 by the anonymous adviser whose argument is recorded in 'Whether it be expedient to make peace with England' (pp. 24–6), referring to a proposed triple alliance based on balance-of-power considerations. Such a principle was satisfactory when the alliance consisted of three out of the four powers which he considered in the situation. Indeed, a contemporary observer noted that the western balance in the early seventeenth century consisted of no more than three powers—Spain, France and England.[11] Thus the competing parties in fact dominated the society at large or the overall framework. But with the expansion of the state-system it would become harder to distil the common necessity or interest. Indeed a sceptical writer like Rousseau was doubtful whether such a thing existed apart from the coincidence of interests occasioned by conflict. He wrote in *The Social Contract* that

> the agreement of all interests is formed by opposition to that of each. If there were no different interests, the common interest would be barely felt, as it would encounter no obstacle: all would go on of its own accord, and politics would cease to be an art.[12]

On this reasoning it follows that the only system-wide coincidence of interests would be the result of a danger of such magnitude that all were threatened equally, in other words a massive hegemonial attempt, either from within or without the system. It was this danger on which the balance-of-power principle was based. F. S. Northedge and M. J. Grieve put it in these terms: '. . . wherever there exists a number of formally independent states with no common superior to impose its will upon them, all have a tendency to fear the predomin-ance of any single one of them and will tend to form alignments so as to prevent the emergence of the single hegemonial state.' [13]

It was in fact the salience of the Franco-Spanish rivalry in the early modern period which encouraged the development of the theory of the balance of power, as Martin Wight has perceptively observed.[14] For the existence of two dominant powers simplified the calculus of forces: France and Spain alternated roles of threat and response as the relative power of each rose and fell in the sixteenth and seven-teenth centuries. Paruta's account of the episode of Leo X, for example, is dominated by the Franco-Spanish rivalry in Italy, and Rohan in a famous passage describes them as 'the two Poles, from whence descend the influence of peace and war upon the other states' (p. 35). It is this structure which underlies Fénelon's fourth type of system in which two equal Powers maintain the balance, though it is somewhat idealized in terms of 'a regard to the public security' (p. 44).

These two dominant 'poles' favoured the application of Newtonian concepts and principles to the 'mechanics' of the balance of power. Felix Gilbert has aptly summed up this conception:

> The individual state would be called a gravitation center which formed a system by attracting smaller states; these 'move in the orbit' of the larger power. Like planets, the great powers would take their own course, sweeping in their wake a number of satellites.

> The great powers would be kept within a calculable orbit because
> they would meet other systems which they were not strong enough
> to attract, but strong enough to resist.[15]

Other physical images occur in these selections. Of particular interest
is the simile of the arch which appears in Gentili (p. 14) and Fénelon
(p. 42): the latter interestingly observes that 'all the stones sustain
each other in pushing against each other'. Another suggestive image
is the 'lattice' or 'network' in the extract from Clausewitz's *On
War* (pp. 104–6); a field of tension and forces provides a framework
for his analysis of the relationship between individual and general
interests.

It is easy to criticize these analogies as static, and other organic
ones as overstressing the solidarity of the community of states. The
criticisms are to some extent well founded, but it should be realized
that one can only work within the conceptions of nature which are
prevalent at the time. It should also be recalled that the pervasiveness
of natural analogies was derived from a tradition of thought which
assumed the universality of the Laws of Nature. Human affairs were
part of nature and subject to its laws; to this extent the analogies
were more apparent than real. This commingling of the natural and
social realms pervades most Enlightenment writings on the balance
of power from Fénelon onwards.

What is one to do, however, when the appeal to the 'natural order
and the light of reason' (Botero) no longer carries great conviction?
How is one to respond to Rousseau (pp. 74–80), who confirmed the
natural bases of the balance of power while revealing the turmoil
and agitation to which it led in the relations among states? Part of the
difficulty arose in the eighteenth century with the decline of the
Hapsburg-Bourbon rivalry as the central axis of the state-system.
Without this clear 'relationship of major tension'[16] the political
calculus was more difficult, though it still worked well at a super-
ficial level in the final decades before the outbreak of the French
Revolution. This was as much due to what F. H. Hinsley calls the
'fortuitous balanced distribution' of the late eighteenth century as
to anything else.[17] But what marked a turning point in the evolution
of the principle of the balance of power was the partition of Poland,
or more accurately, the three partitions of Poland in the late eighteenth century by Austria, Prussia and Russia, who invoked the
balance of power to justify their actions. In the destruction of a
member of the European state-system there seemed to be no harmony
between the individual and collective interest, no creative tension
between opposites balancing each other to preserve the liberties of

Europe. For many, though by no means all, statesmen and publicists, Frederick the Great's couplet in a letter of 1749 to Voltaire would have sounded hollow:

> Et par les poids égaux d'un prudent équilibre
> Elle maintient l'Europe indépendente et libre.[18]

The ramifications of the Polish question during the following century were crucial both in the history of the European state-system and the literature on the balance of power; many of the writings in this anthology reflect this.

The intellectual justification of the balance of power in natural law terms proved to be durable. Edmund Burke's advocacy of the balance of power was based on a naturalistic conception,[19] and Frederick Ancillon wrote of the necessity of 'opposing forces to forces, of counter-balancing action by reaction, of maintaining order, harmony and repose in the world of bodies politic, by the same means which main-tain order, harmony and repose in the physical world, and of trying to bring about equilibrium by skilfully combined attractions and repulsions'.[20] As late as 1864 Lord Palmerston declared in the House of Commons that the balance of power 'is a doctrine founded on the nature of man'.[21]

On the whole, however, after the partition of Poland it became increasingly implausible to assume that the interests of the competing parties would be reconciled naturally with those of the society at large. That Britain was largely disinterested and France helpless in preventing the disappearance of Poland exposed the logical fissures which had always existed in the system of the balance of power. If the natural motions of the system are unable to prevent such a spoliation, what is one to put in their place to keep that fruitful tension between individual and common interests within bounds? Clearly there must be a shift from an order whose rationale is derived from nature's invariable laws to one which is predominantly 'arranged' or 'con-structed'. The transition from a naturalistic to an artificial concep-tion of the balance of power is a gradual one and to some extent parallels the transition from natural to positive theories of inter-national law. It was indeed the development of what became known as 'the public law of Europe' which provided considerable support for the balance-of-power idea. As Martin Wight has observed, the balance of power 'aspired towards the condition of law. It became the first article of the unwritten constitution of the state-system.'[22] There had of course been a long-standing tendency to view the European state-system as analogous to a domestic republic or commonwealth, in the theory of which the balance of power had also figured. In addition to the 'unwritten constitution', the balance of power played an increasing role in the general peace settlements after major coalition wars such as the Thirty Years' War and the War of the Spanish Succession. From the treaties of Utrecht onwards references to the balance become more and more frequent. A compiler of nineteenth-century treaties was so struck by this fact that he commented: 'That these Engagements have been contracted, in many instances, with the avowed object of maintaining the Balance of Power, may be readily tested by referring to the Index under that heading.' [23]

Another element of artificial arrangement which gradually gained prominence in the principle of the balance of power was the role of the balancer. This was an old conception, of course, and one which is implicit in many of the earliest accounts of the balance of power. The long-standing claimant to this role was England. The somewhat crude maxim 'cui adhaereo praeest' ('the party I support wins'), attributed to Henry VIII, is often cited as the first intimation of this role, but Bacon's description in *The Advancement of Learning* (Latin version, 1623) is more suggestive:

> Then follows the reign of a king whose actions, although managed with more vigour than prudence, yet had considerable influence on the affairs of Europe, at one time, by balancing them, and at another causing them to sink in proportion to the weight they [Henry VIII's actions] put into the scale.[24]

It was in relation to the dominant Franco-Spanish rivalry that England's self-portrayal as the balancer gained such an impetus. Halifax gives a boastful description in *The Character of a Trimmer* (1688):

> There was a time when England was the over-balancing power of Christendom, and that either by inheritance or conquest the better part of France received laws from us. After that, we being reduced into our own limits, France and Spain became rivals for the universal monarchy, and our third power, though in itself less than either of the others, happened to be superior to any of them, by that choice we had of throwing the scales on that side to which we gave our friendship, and I do not know whether this figure did not make us as great as our former conquest.[25]

Although the tradition of England as holding the balance has taken on almost mythical proportions, there are many who believe that the notion of balancer is central to the whole balance-of-power idea. 'A real balance of power,' writes Garrett Mattingly, 'requires at least two groups, so evenly matched that neither can easily defeat the other, with a third holding the balance between them'.[26] While the third-party perspective is present in the early allusions to such figures as Lorenzo de' Medici, Henry VIII, the Papacy, Venice, and others, it only really gained a theoretical foothold after it was realized that what Frederick the Great called '*un équilibre de puissances . . . qui constitue une égalite de force entre l'agresseur et l'attaqué*' [27] was no longer sufficient to maintain the independence of states such as Poland. This could only be done, it was widely believed, by a country such as England who, in Sir Eyre Crowe's words, 'has a direct and positive interest in the maintenance of the independence of nations, and therefore must be the natural enemy of any country threatening the independence of others, and the natural protector of the weaker communities'.[28]

A related element in the evolving theory of the balance of power was the principle of intervention, for it was assumed that the balancing role might entail interference in the domestic affairs of foreign states in order to prevent an undue increase in power. This was always a controversial feature of the balance of power, for it seemed to violate the very independence which was the principal objective of the system. Although the prevention of any undue increase in power by conquest was justifiable, it was less easy to justify the prevention of internal growth and development. This of course became an increasingly important issue after the beginning of the Industrial Revolution when comparative rates of industrialization would come to play a greater role in assessments of relative power.

The principal rationale of intervention was the maxim that intentions were to be judged by power, that overweening power no matter how acquired would be a threat to the system. In Ancillon's words 'the measure of forces is the measure of actions, and one must fear everything from one who can undertake everything'.[29] But as the analyses of the state-system became more sophisticated a distinction between conservative and hegemonial powers emerged. England, for instance, was assumed to be in the former category. According to Vattel (pp. 72–3), 'England, whose wealth and powerful navy have given her a very great influence, without, however, causing any State to fear for its liberty, since that power appears to be cured of the spirit of conquest—England, I say, has the honour to hold in her hands the political scales'. Similarly, Bismarck's newly unified German *Reich* did not seem to the makers of British foreign policy to pose a threat to the European balance of power.[30] They might well have recalled Fénelon's warning that a moderate prince in a powerful state would probably be succeeded by a less moderate one (p. 45).

While Vergennes and others severely condemned the partition of Poland on the grounds that it upset the 'general equilibrium' to the benefit of the three partitioning Powers, they generally overlooked an aspect of the affair which was in the long run to become more significant. The eighteenth century has been aptly called the age of partition, but what was distinctively new about the partitions of Poland was the concerted action by the three major Powers involved. In effect this was a forerunner of what was to become known as the Concert of Europe after the Congress of Vienna, at which the pleni-potentiaries of the Great Powers met to re-create Europe on the basis of the principles of equilibrium and legitimacy. Although the soli-darity and co-operation of the Concert of Europe have often been exaggerated,[31] it recognized at least in theory that the balance of power required a more conscious, rational management than the *ad hoc* coalitions which since the late seventeenth century had only prevented the equilibrium from being completely overturned at the last minute. As Leonard Krieger writes, 'In actuality the European concert and the balance of its several sovereign states would be per-manent complements and mutual dependants in the great-power system which would dominate world history from the mid-eighteenth to the mid-twentieth century'.[32]

It is ironic that the increased awareness of the need for diplomatic manipulation to maintain the balance of power came at a time when the easy availability of the traditional counter-weights in the system was disappearing. For the territorial patchwork on which the 'balance of compensation' was based was gradually evolving into a system of sovereign peoples or nations. Alluding no doubt to the Statistics Committee at the Congress of Vienna, Talleyrand argued in the letter reproduced here (p. 100) that 'it would be a very strange mistake to regard as unique elements of the equilibrium the quantities enumerated by political arithmeticians'. It was the very artificiality of the classical eighteenth-century balance-of-power system which was decried by some. In 1804 Prince Adam Czartoryski, in secret instructions from Alexander I to an envoy going to England, argued that the general pacification must not only follow natural boundaries and economic units in fixing the proper limits to different countries. 'It would be necessary at the same time', he added, 'to compose each State of homogeneous peoples, who can agree among themselves and harmonize with the government which rules them. The commo-tions which Europe has continually experienced for so many centuries have largely been caused by the fact that this natural equilibrium has been totally discarded.' [33] As liberal publicists and statesmen in the nineteenth century became more attached to this principle of order, the balancing device of intervention in the domestic affairs of other states became less justifiable in their eyes; in England the doctrine of the balance of power came to be replaced by that of non-intervention, as Reeve's 1875 article in the *Encylopaedia Britannica* (pp. 117–18) maintains. On the other hand, the German writers Leopold von Ranke and Heinrich von Treitschke found little difficulty in combining the idea of separate national development and the balance of power. Von Treitschke assumed, for example, that when great states are strong enough to be self-sufficient they are anxious to secure peace, 'for the safety of their own existence and the civilization of which they are the guardians'; he maintained that 'any organized system of States must assume that no one state is so powerful as to be able to permit itself any licence without danger to itself'.[34] This was to be repudiated by Bismarck's successors. In 1912 General Friedrich von Bernhardi wrote: 'Above all the principle of the European balance of power, which has since the Congress of Vienna led a somewhat sacrosanct but completely unjustified existence, must be completely crushed.' Von Bernhardi wanted to replace the European state-system with a 'world state-system, in which the balance of power was to be constructed on true power factors'.[35] He failed to realize, however, that the European balance-of-power system could not be swept away but had to be accommodated in the emerging global system; it was only in 1945 that this evolutionary process was completed. In the penultimate extract (pp. 128–34) the American diplomat Lewis Einstein provides a more balanced picture of this relationship on the eve of the First World War, in an article which impressed President Theodore Roosevelt.

Perhaps the balance-of-power principle was too closely associated with the *ancien régime* for it to survive the age of nationalism unscathed. 'The equilibrium favourable to peace,' warned Mazzini, 'the so-called balance of power, is an ineffective lie if it is not an equilibrium and balance of justice: to establish it we must have a revision of these unjust, unequal, tyrannical conventions, in which the people are never involved or which they never confirm.' [36] Yet throughout the nineteenth century and into the twentieth century diplomacy and statecraft remained in the hands of an aristocratic *élite* who clung to the traditional ideas of the balance of power and *raison d'état*.

The staying power of the naturalistic conception of the balance of power is illustrated by the generalizations of two modern historians: the last three decades of the century have been described by A. J. P.

Taylor as a period in which the balance of power 'took on the appearance of a natural law, self-operating and self-adjusting', [37] and F. H.
Hinsley asserts that states in the same era 'came to believe that in
foreign affairs, as in such matters as tariffs, the maximum liberty for
each would automatically produce the best results for all'.[38] Underlying conditions, however, were no longer suitable for such a *laissez-
faire* notion of the balance of power. Bertrand Russell, for example,
has emphasized the discrepancy between the high level of organization within states and the virtually complete lack of organization
between states; [39] but perhaps the best statement of the underlying
tension in the pre-war era is to be found in the selection from Winston
Churchill's *The World Crisis* (pp. 134–8).

It is true that the 'balance of compensation' still worked tolerably
well in the realm of colonial expansion, and that the art of diplomatic
manipulation reached new heights with Bismarck's statecraft.
Rousseau's opinion in the *Project for Perpetual Peace* still seemed valid:
'The present system of Europe has its support, in great measure, in
the play of political negotiations, which almost always balance each
other.' Yet as crisis piled upon crisis in the pre-1914 period there
seemed to be absent that just admixture of freedom and constraint
so admirably expressed by Michael Howard:

> International order . . . is based on the understanding by nations
> that their capacity to impose and extend their own favoured order
> is limited by the will and effective ability of other states to impose
> theirs. The conduct of international relations must therefore always
> be a delicate adjustment of power to power, a mutual exploration
> of intentions and capabilities, so as to find and preserve an order
> which, though fully satisfying to nobody, is just tolerable to all.[40]

There has been much debate on the continuing relevance of the
balance-of-power idea, an issue which is beyond the scope of this
primarily historical anthology. Yet it is difficult to deny that Michael
Howard has summed up the principal legacy of the tradition of
balance-of-power statecraft, and that this practical wisdom still
remains valid in the relations among independent political communities.

1 The *locus classicus* is E. W. Nelson, 'The Origins of Modern Balance-of-Power Politics', *Medievalia et Humanistica*, vol. i (1943), pp. 124–42.

2 G. Pillinini, *Il Sistema degli stati italiani 1454–1494* (Venice, 1970). Cf. M. P. Gilmore, *The World of Humanism 1453–1516* (New York, 1952), pp. 139–45.

3 See especially R. Palmarocchi, *La politica italiana di Lorenzo de' Medici* (Florence, 1933), and N. Valeri, *L'Italia nell'età dei principati dal 1343 al 1516* (Milan, 1969).

4 Pillinini, op. cit., p. 52.

5 This phrase is used by G. Quazza, 'La politica dell'equilibrio nel secolo XVIII', in *Nuove questioni di storia moderna* (Milan, 1964), vol. ii, p. 1186.

6 J. P. F. Ancillon, *Tableau des révolutions du système politique de l'Europe* (Paris, 1823), vol. i, p. 262 (first published in 1803–5).

7 J. G. Fichte, *The Characteristics of the Present Age* (translated from the German by William Smith), 2nd ed. (London, 1859), p. 211; reprinted in the present anthology, p. 89.

8 *Vite di uomini illustri*, ed. P. d'Ancona and E. Aeschlimann (Milan, 1951), p. 428.

9 B. Rucellarii, *De Bello Italico . . .* (1724), p. 4.

10 *A World Restored* (New York, 1964), pp. 146–7.

11 Sir Thomas Overbury, writing in 1609, quoted by M. Wight, 'The Balance of Power and International Order' in A. James, ed., *The Bases on International Order* (1973), p. 93.

12 Rousseau, *The Social Contract* (Everyman's University Library No. 660), p. 185n.

13 *A Hundred Years of International Relations* (1971), p. 13.

14 Wight, loc. cit., p. 94.

15 F. Gilbert, *The Beginnings of American Foreign Policy* (New York, 1965), p. 99.

16 A. Wolfers, *Discord and Collaboration* (Baltimore, Md., 1962), p. 101.

17 *Nationalism and the International System* (1973), p. 82.

18 Quoted by H. Gollwitzer, *Europabild und Europagedanke* (Munich, 1964), p. 76. (*Elle = la politique.*)

19 See Hans-Gerd Schumann, *Edmund Burkes Anschauungen vom Gleichgewicht in Staat und Staatensystem* (Meisenheim am Glan, 1964).

20 Ancillon, op. cit., vol. i, p. 32.

21 Quoted by K. Bourne, *The Foreign Policy of Victorian England, 1830–1902* (Oxford, 1970), p. 379.

22 Wight, loc. cit., p. 102.

23 E. Hertslet, *The Map of Europe by Treaty*, quoted by D. P. Heatley, *Diplomacy and the Study of International Relations* (Oxford, 1919), p. 147.

24 Bacon, *Works*, ed. Spedding *et al.* (1857–9), vol. i, p. 509. This translation, by M. R. Wright, is more accurate than that of Spedding, *ibid.*, vol. iv, p. 306.

25 *Halifax: Complete Works*, ed. J. P. Kenyon (Harmondsworth, Mddx., 1969), pp. 86–7.

26 *Renaissance Diplomacy* (1955), p. 163.

27 Frederick the Great, *Die Politischen Testamente*, quoted by H. Butterfield, 'The Balance of Power', in M. Wight and H. Butterfield (eds), *Diplomatic Investigations* (1966), p. 144.

28 'Memorandum on the Present State of British Relations with France and Germany, January 1, 1907', *British Documents on the Origins of the War 1898–1914*, ed. G. P. Gooch and H. Temperley (1928), vol. iii, p. 403.

29 Ancillon, op. cit., vol. i, p. 33.

30 Charles Webster, *The Art and Practice of Diplomacy* (1961), pp. 23–4.

31 O. Halecki provides a contrary assessment: 'The so-called "Concert" of the great European powers was in no sense a permanent organization; guided only by considerations of power politics and expediency, it succeeded in resolving by appeasement several minor conflicts of interests, but it failed—or, rather, it seemed to be non-existent—when the general tension had reached its climax.' *The Limits and Divisions of European History* (London and New York, 1950) pp., 196–7.

32 *Kings and Philosophers 1689–1789* (1971), p. 276.

33 *Mémoires de prince Adam Czartoryski . . .* (Paris, 1887), vol. ii, p. 36.

34 *Politics*, trans. by B. Dugdale & T. de Bille (1916), vol. ii, p. 593.

35 Von Bernhardi, *Deutschland und der nächste Krieg* (Berlin, 1912), quoted by H. Wagner, 'Der "Kontinentalismus" als aussenpolitische Doktrin der USA and ihre historischen Analogien in Europa', *Das Parlament* (Beilage), B23/70, 6th June 1970, p. 33.

36 Quazza, loc. cit., p. 1210.

37 *New Cambridge Modern History*, vol. xi, p. 542.

38 ibid., p. 43.

39 *Freedom versus Organization, 1776–1914* (1965), p. 237.

40 *Studies in War and Peace* (1970), p. 208.

Select Bibliography

TWENTIETH-CENTURY STUDIES AND COLLECTIONS

Anderson, M. S. *The Ascendancy of Europe.* 1972.

Anderson, M. S. 'Eighteenth-Century Theories of the Balance of Power', in R. Hatton and M. S. Anderson (eds), *Studies in Diplomatic History.* 1970. pp. 183–98.

Beloff, M. *The Balance of Power.* Montreal, 1967.

Butterfield, H., and Wight, M. (eds). *Diplomatic Investigations.* 1966.

Claude, I. L. *Power and International Relations.* New York, 1962.

Dehio, L. *The Precarious Balance.* New York, 1962; London, 1963.

Donnadieu, L. *Essai sur la théorie de l'équilibre.* Paris, 1900.

Dupuis, C. *Le principe d'équilibre et le concert européen.* Paris, 1909.

Forsyth, M. G., *et al.* (eds). *The Theory of International Relations.* 1970.

Gareau, F. H. (ed.). *The Balance of Power and Nuclear Deterrence.* Boston, 1962.

Gulick, E. V. *Europe's Classical Balance of Power.* Ithaca, N.Y., and London, 1955.

Haas, E. B. 'The Balance of Power: Prescription, Concept, or Propaganda?' *World Politics,* vol. v (1952–3). pp. 442–77.

Halecki, O. *The Limits and Divisions of European History.* London and New York, 1950.

Hinsley, F. H. *Power and the Pursuit of Peace.* Cambridge, 1963.

Holborn, H. *The Political Collapse of Europe.* New York, 1951.

Holbraad, C. *The Concert of Europe.* 1970.

Kaeber, E. *Die Idee des europäischen Gleichgewichts in der publizistischen Literatur vom 16. bis zur Mitte des 18. Jahrhunderts.* Berlin, 1907.

Kissinger, H. A. *A World Restored.* Boston, 1957; New York, 1964.

Liska, G. *International Equilibrium.* Cambridge, Mass., 1957.

Mattingly, G. *Renaissance Diplomacy.* 1955.

Maurseth, P. 'Balance-of-Power Thinking from the Renaissance to the French Revolution'. *Journal of Peace Research,* No. 2 (1964). pp. 120–36.

Morandi, C. 'Il concetto della politica d' equilibrio nell'Europa moderna'. *Archivio Storico Italiano,* vol. 98 (1940). pp. 3–19.

Morgenthau, H. J., and Thompson, K. W. (eds). *Principles and Problems of International Politics.* New York, 1950.

Mowat, R. B. *The European States System.* 1923.

Nelson, E. W. 'The Origins of Modern Balance-of-Power Politics'. *Medievalia et Humanistica*, vol. i (1943). pp. 124–42.

Pillinini, G. *Il Sistema degli stati italiani 1454–1494.* Venice, 1970.

Quazza, G. 'La politica dell'equilibrio nel secolo XVIII'. *Nuove questioni di storia moderna*, vol. ii (Milan, 1964). pp. 1181–215.

Seabury, P. (ed.). *Balance of Power.* San Francisco, 1965.

Strang, Lord. *Britain in World Affairs.* 1961.

Vagts, A. 'The Balance of Power: Growth of an Idea'. *World Politics*, vol. i (1948–9). pp. 82–101.

Von Vietsch, E. *Das europäische Gleichgewicht.* Leipzig, 1942.

Wight, M. 'The Balance of Power and International Order'. *The Bases of International Order*, A. James (ed.). 1973. pp. 85–115.

Wolf, J. B. *Toward a European Balance of Power 1620–1715.* Chicago, 1970.

Wolfers, A., and Martin, L. W. (eds). *The Anglo-American Tradition in Foreign Affairs.* New Haven, Conn. and London, 1956.

Wright, Q. *A Study of War*, vol. ii, ch. 20. Chicago, 1942.

Zeller, G. 'Le principe d'équilibre dans la politique internationale avant 1789'. *Revue historique*, vol. 215 (1956). pp. 25–37.

WRITINGS ON THE BALANCE OF POWER BEFORE 1914 NOT REPRESENTED IN THIS ANTHOLOGY

Ancillon, J. P. F. *Tableau des révolutions du système politique de l'Europe depuis la fin du quinzième siècle.* Berlin, 1803–5.

Anon. *An Appendix to the Memoirs of the Duke de Ripperda.* 1740.

Bacon, Francis. *Works* (1857–9), and *Letters and Life* (1861–74).

Bethel, Slingsby. *The World's Mistake in Oliver Cromwell.* . . . 1668; reprinted by *The Rota*, University of Exeter, 1972.

Bolingbroke, Viscount. *Letters on the Study and Use of History.* 1752.

Botero, G. *The Reason of State* (translated from the Italian edition of 1598). 1956.

Burrows, M. 'The Balance of Power'. *Quarterly Review*, vol. 143 (1877). pp. 526–50.

Brougham, Lord. *An Inquiry into the Colonial Policy of the European Powers.* Edinburgh, 1803.

Brougham, Lord. *Works*, vol. viii, Dissertations—Historical and Political. Edinburgh, 1872.

Burke, Edmund. *Thoughts on the Prospect of a Regicide Peace.* 1796.

Burke, Edmund. 'Thoughts on French Affairs' and 'Remarks on the Policy of the Allies with Respect to France'. *Three Memorials on French Affairs* (1797).

Carné-Marcien, L. 'De l'équilibre européen . . .' *Revue des deux mondes*, 4th series, vol. 24 (1840). pp. 465–95.

Crowe, Sir Eyre. 'Memorandum on the Present State of British Relations with France and Germany, January 1, 1907'. G. P. Gooch and H. Temperley (eds), *British Documents on the Origins of the War 1898–1914*, vol. iii (1928).

Davenant, Charles. *Essays upon: 1. The Balance of Power.* . . . 1701.

Defoe, Daniel. *The ballance of Europe.* 1711.

Defoe, Daniel. *Review.* 1704–13. (Facsimile edition: New York, 1938.)

Dottain, E. 'Des variations du système d'équilibre en Europe'. *Revue contemporaine*, 2nd series, vol. 20 (1861). pp. 128–50.

Favier, J. L. *Politique de tous les cabinets de l'Europe.* Paris, 1793, 1801, 1802.

Frantz, G. A. C. *Untersuchungen über das Europäische Gleichgewicht.* Berlin, 1859.

Frederick the Great. 'Considerations on the Present State of the Body-Politic in Europe' (translated from the French of 1736). *Posthumous Works of Frederick II*, vol. iv (1789).

Halifax, Marquess of. *The Character of a Trimmer.* 1688. Reprinted in *Halifax: Complete Works* (Pelican Classics). 1969.

Heeren, A. H. L. *A Manual of the History of the Political System of Europe and its Colonies* (translation of the 5th German edition of 1830). Oxford, 1834.

Hertzberg, M. le comte de. *Huit dissertations.* . . . Berlin, 1787.

Justi, J. H. von. *Die Chimäre des Gleichgewichts von Europa.* Altona, 1758.

Kahle, L. M. *La Balance de l'Europe considérée comme la règle de la paix et de la guerre.* Berlin-Göttingen, 1744.

Kant, I. *Perpetual Peace; a Philosophical Essay* (translated from the German of 1795). 1903.

Lisola, F. P. de. *Le bouclier d'estat et de justice.* The Hague, 1667.

Mackintosh, Sir James. 'Speech on the Annexation of Genoa to the Kingdom of Sardinia', 27th April 1815. *Miscellaneous Works* (1851).

Metternich, Prince de. *Mémoires, documents et écrits divers.* . . . Paris, 1880–4.

Napier, Macvey. 'The Balance of Power'. *Encyclopaedia Britannica*, Supplement (1824), 7th edition (1842), 8th edition (1854).

Nys, E. 'La théorie de l'équilibre européen'. *Revue de droit international et de législation comparée*, vol. 25 (1893). pp. 34–57.

Pitt, William. 'Official Communication made to the Russian Ambassador at London, on the 19th January, 1805. . . .' C. K. Webster. *British Diplomacy 1813–1815* (1921). pp. 389–94.

Pufendorf, S. *An Introduction to the History of the Principal Kingdoms and States of Europe.* 1697.

Von Ranke, L. 'The Great Powers'. Theodore von Laue. *Leopold von Ranke: The Formative Years* (Princeton, 1950).

Rohan, Henri de. *Mémoires.* Amsterdam, 1756.

Simpson, J. Y. *The Saburov Memoirs, or, Bismarck and Russia. . . .* Cambridge, 1929.

Sorel, A. *Europe and the French Revolution* (translated from the French edition of 1885). 1969.

Treitschke, H. von. *Politics* (translated from lectures given in Berlin in 1874), vol. ii. 1916.

Voltaire. *The Age of Louis XIV.* 1926. (Everyman's Library No. 780.)

Unless otherwise stated the place of publication of works, both here and throughout the book, is London

Chronology

The Italian Origins

LORENZO DE' MEDICI
TWO LETTERS ON FLORENTINE DIPLOMACY

[From: *Scritti scelti di Lorenzo de' Medici*. Ed. Emilio Bigi. Turin 1955. pp. 653–6, 667–70. Translated by John Warrington.]

Lorenzo de' Medici (1449–1492) governed Florence from 1469 until his death, though without holding any formal office. Probably the most widely accomplished of the Medici family, Lorenzo skilfully managed Florentine diplomacy in an era when Florence's central location and the financial resources of the Medicis gave her a pivotal role in the Italian system. These two letters to his diplomatic envoys are difficult because of the complexity of the *pratiche* (intrigues) with which they deal and the indirectness of Lorenzo's approach to them. They reveal Lorenzo's concern with relative strengths and countervailing power arrangements, although there is little awareness of the balance-of-power idea as such. They also suggest that the so-called balance-of-power era in the latter half of the fifteenth century was less serene than later commentators, such as Guicciardini in the following selection, claim in idealizing Lorenzo's statecraft.

LORENZO DE' MEDICI TO IACOPO GUICCIARDINI[1]

Florence, 26th July 1486

. . . Now we see what some have long understood, that the Pope and the Doge of Genoa have been playing a game, and as regards the Venetians we have an idea that if our words had been heard and remembered, these matters would have a better ending. The length of the King's war, which might at the beginning have been shortened, has had the usual result of long illnesses: they give rise to ailments different from the original and sometimes kill the patient. When this war started it could not have been foreseen that the Duke of Lorraine's threat would add to the King's trouble, and only now one can see that it might be his death.

We have left the Venetians and Genoa to Signor Lodovico's care, as he wished. It grieves me that all of us are deceived; it is better to correct than to punish, and at present two remedies are needed. First, to change the régime of Genoa, which here and now is the best thing that could happen. Second, I think it necessary that these galleys of ours should at once send a large sum of money to the field of operations from that gentleman [Lodovico] and ourselves—surely not less than 30,000 ducats—because, if Genoa arms herself, either we shall lose, or we shall retreat and the Orsini's dominions will remain in suspense, which means in effect that the Orsini will reach agreement with the Pope, with the inevitable consequences. Sufficient money must therefore be sent to pay the mercenaries and the Regular army for two or three months, allowing, I think, for at least 3,000 infantry to guard the conquered territory and the field of operations, above all because I think it will be necessary for the Duke of Calabria with some of his people to return to the Kingdom. I believe that by doing these two things we shall have time to see how powerful he [the Duke of Lorraine] becomes and how the Venetians behave, and we shall be able to decide according to events. Otherwise we shall not be able to wait long and any decision we take will involve loss of reputation and security. It seems to me essential that Signor Lodovico be clearly understood; and in order to understand him we must see if he is willing to provide the above-mentioned sum, for this is a cause worthy of his treasures and of his heart, if nothing else.

You know, Iacopo, that I have often told you what you know much better than I do, namely what a grievous burden I have to carry because of the slowness of those provisions and the way in which they are carried out. Think of all the inconveniences that will fall on me if he [Lodovico] dies; for you know better than I the people's humour, the good-will the French bear towards us, and the malevolence of others. If everything possible is done about this matter, and wholeheartedly, I shall have no fear; if I limp a little, I should not like to remain there without some help, especially as there are

some who think this could easily happen. I should not like to
have to deal with so many things, because what I have already
done seems too much. I think all this must be explained to
Signor Lodovico, for I should not like you to entrust me with
something I could not do.

You have seen the articles drawn up at Rome on the 18th.
But I think that if the Duke of Lorraine comes, we could not
trust him even if the Pope were to declare peace; you understand why better than I do. I don't know what you think about
it; for my part I think that his coming would make little
difference between peace and war . . .

I think it will be necessary to reach an understanding with
the Venetians, by showing them that what has hitherto been
done here in the King's favour has been done so that the
Church's power may not increase to such an extent as to rule
both them and ourselves. Now, assuming the Duke of Lorraine's arrival, we should like to know the intentions of the
Venetian government, whether it proposes to be for or against
or neutral, because it might be able to take a decision which
the others would follow. In fact, I do not see that one king or
another makes much difference, so long as that state [Venice]
does not join the States of the Church.

I say this because, if the Venetians do not like this transalpine power in Italy, they should make themselves quite
clear, especially as we can sooner and more easily establish
the Duke of Lorraine in the Kingdom than the Pope and the
Venetians can together. I really would like the Venetians to
understand that if they are willing to take measures against
this danger which still threatens us, they may, when they
desire something else, rely upon us to do all we can, no matter
how insupportable the burden.

That is what I want. I think Lodovico should be made to
understand these things clearly, as any perplexity or doubt
at this time could result in the gravest inconveniences. We
must therefore quickly make up our minds as to what decision
should be taken, and that decision must involve no half-
measures. I think that any decision will be less reprehensible
if, with the trust that should exist between that state and ourselves, we act freely and in unison as we firmly intend to do.

It seems to me that no such grave events have occurred for a very long time, and that now, in face of so many troubles and inconveniences, we must take a decision.

[1] Lorenzo wrote this letter to his envoy in Milan two weeks before the end of the King of Naples' war against his rebellious barons, who were supported by Pope Innocent VIII and Venice. Lorenzo's concerns at this stage were to keep intact the Florence-Milan-Naples alliance, to mediate between the two sides, and to avoid intervention by the Duke of Lorraine with French troops on the Pope's side. The more immediate problem discussed in this letter is Genoa's attempt to trick Lodovico and hold him in check, and the fate of the Orsini, who it was feared might go over to the Pope's side.

LORENZO DE' MEDICI TO GIOVANNI LANFREDINI[1]

Florence, 17th October 1489

I understand from yours of the 13th that Our Lordship has taken some offence at your request that these citations should go no further. I regret offence to His Holiness, but I should be particularly grieved if he suspected that my words or actions were due to any cause other than the welfare of His Holiness, who may be assured that in every situation and on every occasion I wish, as a servant, to support that same welfare. To that principle I hold firm forever. If I have urged His Holiness to be moderate in these proceedings against the King, I have done so for the undermentioned reasons. As I said in my last letter, it seems to me necessary for His Holiness to adopt one of the three following aims: to triumph over the King by force; or to come to terms as best he can; or, if that understanding which might at present be made would be less than honourable, to temporize more honourably, waiting for a better chance. The first alternative would be the most honourable; but in my opinion it would be rather dangerous and extremely costly, nor do I believe it could ever be accomplished without introducing a new power into the Kingdom. For this I consider three things to be necessary: first, that at least either Venice or Milan agree to this undertaking; second, that the aforesaid power, newly introduced, be itself equally strong in both purse and people; third, that for Our Lordship, regardless of money or anything else, every possible means ought to be employed to accomplish the enterprise. It is also necessary that between what the Pope can do and what this new power can do, there should be a power greater than that of the King alone, assuming that the adherence of Venice to this arrangement would have the effect of preventing Milan from assisting the King. Anyone who had an understanding with the King's barons, or other similar supporters, would be able to act so much the better. Now, I may have been mistaken at the outset when I dissuaded Our Lordship, because I did not see those conditions fulfilled to the extent I considered sufficient, maybe because I did not know all the secrets of this affair. As far as I can see or understand, that is not the right way, because Our Lordship ought by now to realize that either Spain or France must be chosen for this purpose; and Spain seems to me to have very little power, particularly financial power. In France, having regard to their nature, I do not know how it is possible to lay a foundation, but supposing that that nature were to change, I would agree with Our Lordship that the situation would not be too bad, especially as an increase of power in a member of the house of Lorraine would be less dangerous than in Spain; for the Duke of Lorraine is not the King of France, and we know by experience that the King of Naples has much closer relations with Spain than the Duke of Lorraine has with France. Nevertheless, the King of Naples and Spain are not friends, and anyone who might be King of the Realm would look after his own affairs. For all these reasons I would never encourage Our Lordship to attempt such an undertaking now; and that being so, it is useless to exasperate the King with citations and so forth; rather indeed, anyone who shunned such an enterprise would seem to me to avoid any demonstration of hostility in order to escape the danger of what the King may do in passing from words to deeds. This seems to me no small matter; it would therefore be better to dissimulate and apply oneself to secret preparation than to show ill will before the Pope takes the offensive, which is nothing else than to afford him an excuse for making preparations and striking first. Consequently, in this first situation I have every reason to think it unwise to cite the King. As for the second objective, reaching an agreement, I may perhaps again be deceived because conditions are proposed which are unknown to me, conditions to which this method of citation is more favourable, a method that might be useful when the business has matured and is almost concluded. But if there are no conditions beyond those known to me, the affair seems distasteful and by no means easy to resolve; and so these methods which are employed to further such affairs may perhaps give rise to some scandal or rupture which is the opposite of agreement.

As to temporizing, I think it calls for no argument, because it is incomparably better to settle matters with Our Lordship's reputation intact than to tempt fortune, especially as you know much better than I do that the King is easily offended. Now, as I said above, since I know no more of these matters I cannot tell you anything else. If the Pope's slight anxiety is well founded, let me know and lift this burden of worry from me. Although I am not by nature a coward, the Pope's trust in me causes me much greater anxiety about his affairs than I would have about my own. When His Holiness is assured of this, that I attribute so much to his prudence and authority, I shall be able to relax. So long as I have no other grounds for his security, I confess that my mind is not at rest. If there be such grounds, for God's sake let me know, for I am not at all satisfied. The Pope must have no reason in the world to think that I shall employ any means, by word or deed, to further any particular proposal beyond His Holiness's need, because the benefits I have received and hope to receive from Our Lordship are due entirely to his welfare and reputation. About Signor Lodovico I have said as much as I intend, and have opened my heart on the subject of his character.

I know that I am doing the right thing, and have based my trust on Our Lordship. Nor shall I say anything different from what I have often said, namely that if His Holiness can reach agreement with the King with some degree of honour, it seems better to have a common understanding than a success-ful war. If there were difficulties I would arrange some tempor-ization with honour and safety, subject to those conditions which could avail against the King and which I have mentioned above. Granted those conditions, I feel sure that the King would be amenable and would behave straightforwardly. And because I believe that the King understands very well the harm he might suffer, I doubt whether he will come in great strength.

All these reasons of mine may be worthless. Our Lordship may have secrets unknown to me. I do not think Our Lordship can resent these my words; with this resolve of mine always to experience the same fortune as His Holiness, I want always to have licence to speak freely and to fulfil the wishes of His Holiness . . .

[1] After the peace treaty of 11th August 1486 ended the War of the Barons, relations between Pope Innocent VIII and King Ferdinand of Naples did not return to normal, and on 11th September 1489 the Pope decided to remove from Ferdinand the Church's investiture of feudal domain. This action constitutes the 'citations' which Lorenzo criticizes in this letter to his envoy in Rome. Lorenzo had by this time established closer links with the Pope, which he primarily used in this case to restrain the latter from further adventures which might lead to foreign intervention.

FRANCESCO GUICCIARDINI

[From: *The History of Italy* (1561). Translated by Sidney Alexander. New York 1969. pp. 3–9].

Francesco Guicciardini (1483–1540) had his first experience of Renaissance diplomacy when he was for two years Florentine ambassador to Ferdinand the Catholic, King of Spain. Then for nearly twenty years he served as governor of several of the Papal States, but his pro-French policy contributed to the sack of Rome and led to his downfall. His political fortunes in Florence, too, suffered vicissitudes, particularly with those of the Medici, and he eventually retired to a villa near Florence where, during the last three years of his life, he wrote his monumental *Storia d'Italia*. In the opening pages he draws an idealized portrait of Italy before the catastrophe of the French invasion of 1494, and attributes this happy state of affairs largely to the wise diplomacy of Lorenzo de' Medici. It is this passage which is primarily responsible for Lorenzo's reputation as the first balance-of-power statesman, and should be compared with the two letters by Lorenzo himself.

I have determined to write about those events which have occurred in Italy within our memory, ever since French troops, summoned by our own princes, began to stir up very great dissensions here: a most memorable subject in view of its scope and variety, and full of the most terrible happenings; since for so many years Italy suffered all those calamities with which miserable mortals are usually afflicted, sometimes because of the just anger of God, and sometimes because of the impiety and wickedness of other men. From a knowledge of such occurrences, so varied and so grave, everyone may derive many precedents salutary both for himself and for the public weal. Thus numerous examples will make it plainly evident how mutable are human affairs, not unlike a sea whipped by winds; and how pernicious, almost always to themselves but always to the people, are those ill-advised measures of rulers who act solely in terms of what is in front of their eyes: either foolish errors or shortsighted greed. Thus by failing to take account of the frequent shifts of fortune, and misusing, to the harm of others, the power conceded to them for the common welfare, such rulers become the cause of new perturbations either through lack of prudence or excess of ambition.

But the misfortunes of Italy (to take account of what its condition was like then, as well as the causes of so many troubles) tended to stir up men's minds with all the more displeasure and dread inasmuch as things in general were at that time most favourable and felicitous. It is obvious that ever since the Roman Empire, more than a thousand years ago, weakened mainly by the corruption of ancient customs, began to decline from that peak which it had achieved as a result of marvellous skill and fortune, Italy had never enjoyed such prosperity, or known so favourable a situation as that in which it found itself so securely at rest in the year of our Christian salvation, 1490, and the years immediately before and after. The greatest peace and tranquillity reigned everywhere; the land under cultivation no less in the most mountainous and arid regions than in the most fertile plains and areas; dominated by no power other than her own, not only did Italy abound in inhabitants, merchandise and riches, but she was also highly renowned for the magnificence of many princes, for the splendour of so many most noble and beautiful cities, as the seat and majesty of religion, and flourishing with men most skilful in the administration of public affairs and most nobly talented in all disciplines and distinguished and industrious in all the arts. Nor was Italy lacking in military glory according to the standards of that time, and adorned with so many gifts that she deservedly held a celebrated name and reputation among all the nations.

Many factors kept her in that state of felicity which was the consequence of various causes. But it was most commonly agreed that, among these, no small praise should be attributed to the industry and skill of Lorenzo de' Medici, so eminent amongst the ordinary rank of citizens in the city of Florence that the affairs of that republic were governed according to his counsels. Indeed, the power of the Florentine Republic resulted more from its advantageous location, the abilities of its citizens and the availability of its money than from the extent of its domain. And having recently become related by marriage to the Roman Pontiff, Innocent VIII, who was thus induced to lend no little faith in his advice, Lorenzo's name was held in great esteem all over Italy, and his authority influential in deliberations on joint affairs. Realizing that it would be most perilous to the Florentine Republic and to himself if any of the major powers should extend their area of dominion, he carefully saw to it that the Italian situation should be maintained in a state of balance, not leaning more toward one side than the other. This could not be achieved without preserving the peace and without being diligently on the watch against every incident, even the slightest.

Sharing the same desire for the common peace was the King of Naples, Ferdinand of Aragon, undoubtedly a most prudent and highly esteemed prince, despite the fact that quite often in the past he had revealed ambitions not conducive toward maintaining the peace, and at this time he was being greatly instigated by his eldest son Alfonso, Duke of

Calabria. For the Duke tolerated with ill grace the fact that
his son-in-law, Giovan Galeazzo Sforza, Duke of Milan,
already past twenty, although of very limited intellectual
capacity, kept his dukedom in name only, having been sup-
pressed and supplanted by Lodovico Sforza, his uncle. More
than ten years before, as a result of the reckless and dissolute
behaviour of Donna Bona, the young prince's mother,
Lodovico Sforza had taken tutelage over his nephew and,
using that as an excuse, had little by little gathered into his
own hands all the fortresses, men-at-arms, treasury and
foundations of the state, and now continued to govern, not as
guardian or regent but, except for the title of Duke of Milan,
with all the outward trappings and actions of a prince.

Nevertheless, Ferdinand, more immediately concerned with
present benefits than former ambitions, or his son's grievances,
however justified, desired that Italy should not change. Perhaps
he feared that troubles in Italy would offer the French a
chance to assail the kingdom of Naples, since he himself, a few
years earlier, had experienced amidst the gravest perils the
hatred of his barons and his people, and he knew the affection
which many of his subjects held towards the name of the house
of France in remembrance of things past. Or perhaps he
realized that it was necessary for him to unite with the others,
and especially with the states of Milan and Florence, in order
to create a counterbalance against the power of the Venetians,
who were then formidable in all of Italy.

Lodovico Sforza, despite the fact that he was restless and
ambitious, could not help but incline toward the same policy,
since the danger of the Venetian Senate hung over those who
ruled Milan as well as over the others, and because it was easier
for him to maintain his usurped authority in the tranquillity
of peace rather than in the perturbations of war. And although
he always suspected the intentions of Ferdinand and Alfonso
of Aragon, nevertheless, since he was aware of Lorenzo de'
Medici's disposition toward peace, as well as the fear that
Lorenzo also had of their grandeur, Sforza persuaded himself
that, in view of the diversity of spirit and ancient hatred
between Ferdinand and the Venetians, it would be foolish to
fear that they might set up an alliance between them, and

decided that it was most certain that the Aragonese would not be accompanied by others in attempting against him what they could not achieve by themselves.

Therefore, since the same desire for peace existed among Ferdinand, Lodovico and Lorenzo, in part for the same reasons and in part for different reasons, it was easy to maintain an alliance contracted in the names of Ferdinand, King of Naples, Giovan Galeazzo, Duke of Milan, and the Republic of Florence, in defence of their states. This alliance, which had been agreed upon many years before and then interrupted as a result of various occurrences, had been adhered to in the year 1480 by practically all the minor Italian powers and renewed for twenty-five years. The principal aim of the pact was to prevent the Venetians from becoming any more powerful since they were undoubtedly stronger than any of the allies alone, but much weaker than all of them together. The Venetians continued to follow their own policies apart from common counsels, and while waiting for the growth of disunion and conflicts among the others, remained on the alert, prepared to take advantage of every mishap that might open the way for them toward ruling all of Italy. The fact that they aspired toward Italian hegemony had been very clearly shown at various times; especially, when taking advantage of the death of Filippo Maria Visconti, Duke of Milan, they had tried to become lords of that state, under the pretext of defending the liberty of the Milanese; and more recently when, in open war, they attempted to occupy the duchy of Ferrara.

This alliance easily curbed the cupidity of the Venetian Senate, but it did not unite the allies in sincere and faithful friendship, insofar as, full of emulation and jealousy among themselves, they did not cease to assiduously observe what the others were doing, each of them reciprocally aborting all the plans whereby any of the others might become more powerful or renowned. This did not result in rendering the peace less stable; on the contrary, it aroused greater vigilance in all of them to carefully stamp out any sparks which might be the cause of a new conflagration.

Such, therefore, was the state of affairs, such were the foun-

dations of the tranquillity of Italy, disposed and counterpoised
in such a way that not only was there no fear of any present
change, but neither could anyone easily conceive of any
policies or situations or wars that might disrupt such peace.

But then in April of the year 1492, there unexpectedly
occurred the death of Lorenzo de' Medici: a death bitter for
him in view of his age, inasmuch as he had not yet completed
his forty-fourth year, and bitter for his country which had
flourished marvellously in riches and all those benefits and
arts in human affairs which are the usual concomitants of a
long-lasting peace, all resulting from Lorenzo's reputation and
wisdom and talent for all manner of honourable and excellent
undertakings. His death was indeed most untimely for the
rest of Italy, not only because efforts toward the continuation
of the common security were carried on by hands other than
his, but also because he had been the means of moderating,
and practically a bridle, in the disagreements and suspicions
which very often developed for diverse reasons between
Ferdinand and Lodovico Sforza, princes of almost equal
power and ambition. . . .

ALBERICO GENTILI

[From: *De Iure Belli Libri Tres*, ii. Translation of the edition of 1612 by
John C. Rolfe. Oxford and London 1933. pp. 64–6.]

Alberico Gentili (1552–1608) was a Protestant Italian jurist who
taught law at the University of Oxford for some years. His treatise *De
Iure Belli Libri Tres* (1598) expounded the laws of war in the sixteenth
century in a positivist spirit, though still relying heavily on ancient
authorities; his eulogy of Lorenzo de' Medici is based on Guicciardini.
His main concern in this extract is to establish the justice of efforts
to oppose 'powerful and ambitious chiefs', although he admits that
other reasons may be required as well.

. . . Do not all men with complete justice oppose on one side
the Turks and on the other the Spaniards, who are planning

and plotting universal dominion? True, the Turk does not injure many, nor does the Spaniard; neither one nor the other is able to do so; but they injure some, and he who injures one, threatens many. Shall we wait until they actually take up arms? We have heard about the Turks before and we all have our opinion of them. If any one does not know about the Spaniards, let him learn from Paolo Giovio that their disposition also is lawless and greedy for power; and when they have once crept in, they always secure the supreme control by every kind of artifice.

We must therefore oppose them; and it is better to provide that men should not acquire too great power, than to be obliged to seek a remedy later, when they have already become too powerful. 'While your enemy is weak, slay him. Wickedness should be destroyed in the seed, that it may not yield a crop of weeds.' Why are not these words of St Jerome appropriate here? We must unite in opposing the common danger. A common cause for fear unites even those who are most alien; this is a natural law, quoted by our friend Baldus from Aristotle. 'The purpose of empires is to avoid harm', as Dionysius represents some one as justly saying; and no oracle could have spoken with greater truth, in the opinion of Bodin.

'It is enough to be able to do harm. Destroy in advance whatever can harm others', is the apt expression of a talented poet. In fact, it is very unpleasant to be liable to suffer wrong, even though we may not suffer it, as Plutarch says. And Baldus declares that it is lawful to take action to protect oneself; that it ought not to be in the power of an adversary to injure us if he wishes; and that one should provide, not only against what is harmful, but against what may be harmful. So, too, the maintenance of union among the atoms is dependent upon their equal distribution; and on the fact that one molecule is not surpassed in any respect by another.

This it is which was the constant care of Lorenzo de' Medici, that wise man, friend of peace, and father of peace, namely, that the balance of power should be maintained among the princes of Italy. This he believed would give peace to Italy as indeed it did so long as he lived and preserved that condition of affairs. But both the peace and the balance of power

ended with him, great scion of the Medici and mighty bulwark
of his native city and the rest of Italy. Is not this even to-day
our problem, that one man may not have supreme power and
that all Europe may not submit to the domination of a single
man? Unless there is something which can resist Spain,
Europe will surely fall. 'Just as, if any one should pluck out
the keystone of an arch, on which all the stones lean, the rest
would follow and fall with it.'

No one's sovereignty must ever on any account be allowed
to grow so great, that it is not permitted to call in question
even his manifest injustice, as Polybius says. And he adds that
Hiero aided the Carthaginians in their war against the mercenaries, in order that the Carthaginians might not be crushed
and the Romans control everything. Thus Livy speaks of the
various feelings of men with regard to the contest between
the Romans and Perseus, some favouring one side, and others
the other, while a third party ('the best and wisest') consisted
of those who wished neither nation to become more powerful
through the overthrow of the other. For they thought that
mankind would fare best if the one power constantly furnished
protection against the injustice of the other. And this is admirably expressed by Marcus Cato in his *Oration in behalf of the
Rhodians*, when they, through hatred for the Romans, had
favoured Perseus, at least so far as their good will and prayers
were concerned.

'They would have preferred,' he says, 'that we did not
conquer the king. But so, too, would many other peoples and
nations; and some of them had this feeling, not from a desire
for our humiliation, but because they feared that if there
should be no man of whom we stood in awe, we would do
whatever we chose. In the same way each of us, if he thinks
that anything is being done contrary to his interests, strives
with all his might to prevent its being done.' The envoy of
Perseus had appealed to the Rhodians with this same argument; namely, that they should not allow universal control
and power to fall into the hands of one people.

Cato adds that one ought not to be punished merely
because of his desire to do harm, and this should be obvious.
Cæsar does not contradict him when, speaking of making

war upon Ariovistus, he says that the king ought to be punished before he becomes more powerful and inflicts some injury; that is, because he even thought of doing harm. For these words ought not to be understood of the mere thought and the mere desire, but of an impulse which was accompanied with action, as is made clear elsewhere. That king was already an object of fear to the Romans in Gaul, and his arms threatened danger. Therefore it was wise and just for Caesar to think that there ought to be no delay, but that arms should be held in check by arms. The Swiss recently determined very wisely that they would favour neither France nor the Emperor, but would keep their agreements with both, so long as their arms did not appear dangerous to the Swiss republic.

But to conclude, a defence is just which anticipates dangers that are already meditated and prepared, and also those which are not meditated, but are probable and possible. This last word, however, is not to be taken literally, for in that case my statement would be that it is just to resort to a war of this kind as soon as any one becomes too powerful, which I do not maintain. For what if a prince should have his power increased by successions and elections? Will you assail him in war because his power may possibly be dangerous to you? Some other reason must be added for justice's sake. . . .

PAOLO PARUTA

WHETHER THE OPINION OF POPE LEO THE TENTH WERE GOOD OR NO, AND HIS COUNSEL SAFE, OF DRIVING FOREIGN NATIONS OUT OF ITALY, BY THE HELP OF OTHER TRANSALPINE FORCES (1599). *Extract*

[From: *Politick Discourses* . . . Rendered into English by the Right Honourable Henry, Earl of Monmouth, 1657. pp. 183–5.]

Paolo Paruta (1540–1598), Venetian politician and writer, founded a private academy of political and moral sciences at the age of twentyone. His writings on these subjects paralleled his public career, which

included appointments as governor of Brescia (1591), ambassador
to Rome (1592), and official historian of Venice (from 1579). His
Discorsi politici, published in 1599 and translated into English in
1657, deals with contemporary history and politics in the style of
Machiavelli's *Discorsi*. In the essay of which an extract is printed here,
Paruta argues that Pope Leo X, by joining with Emperor Charles V
(often referred to as Caesar) in an offensive league against France in
1521, did not act in accordance with the principle of balanced
power.

. . . What reason was there then to believe, that when
Caesar should become more powerful in Italy, and should
have driven out the French, he should likewise be expelled
from thence, when his Territories and Authority should be
there the greater? It is rather to be believed, that by his
increase of power, Italy should be in a worse condition, and
the danger thereof the more, for whilst these two Princes
stood upon equal terms, and with an inveterate mind did
counterpoise one another, the other States were the more
secure, it being unlikely that one party would permit that
the other should increase, or be heightened by the ruin of any
of the Princes of Italy; but he that should be assaulted by one
was sure to be assisted by the other. Leo ought chiefly to have
endeavoured in this conjuncture of affairs to have kept these
scales even by his neutrality; for whilst the business stood thus,
it behoved the very Enemies of the Italians to value their
Friendship, for their own good, and for the preservation of their
States.

It is not easy to decide whether it did really conduce more
to the good of Italy, that the Pope should continue in his neutrality, or join with some one of these foreign Princes who at
that time had so great an influence upon Italy. It is inevitable
that the success of such affairs depends on many and various
accidents, all of which human wisdom is unable to provide
against, so there is no secure way which leads to that destined
end. Let us say then (still keeping ourselves within some
general rules) in the first place, that to join in friendship and
confederacy with a more powerful Prince, and one who is a
near neighbor, when an increase of its power is intended by
this conjunction, is never to be done without danger, nor

ought such a resolution ever be taken but out of great necessity; especially not by such Princes, who are not so weak, as they need a leaning stock, nor to depend in all things upon the event of another's fortune. Now Leo had no such reason to forego the little quiet which he had then purchased by plunging into a Sea of very slippery Leagues and Confederacies with Princes of great power, desirous of glory, claiming the same things, and between whom War is not so easily ended, as it is resumed. The Church's Patrimony was sufficiently secured by the majesty of Religion, by Pontifical power, by the monies which by many ways she may be supplied with, and by her Dominions, being at this time much enlarged by Julius II. However, as Leo's intention is to be praised for having his thoughts so carefully bent upon the Liberty of Italy, it is similarly desired that he had had either more judgement or temper, to know and choose an opportune time, and a fitting occasion; and yet it is likewise a general rule, that to wait for the advantage of Time, when Affairs are upon great straits, does usually bring notable advantages, and sometimes by new and unexpected ways.

Italy was long under the obedience of the Western Emperors. If at that time when their power and authority was so great, the Popes would have called in foreign Forces, and made use of them to reduce the Government of Italy under the Church's power, or else into the hands of some other Italian Princes, Italy would in the first place have certainly been given in prey to the insolence of foreign Soldiers, and at last she would peradventure have been brought to a worse condition. But by temporizing, such occasions arose, as the Church increased her Dominions by certain lawful Donations without the shedding of blood, and all Italy remained subject to her own proper and particular Lords; and the Western Emperors being long vexed and troubled by the Wars of Germany, were forced to forego the affairs of Italy.

Moreover, though Caesar's fortune and power was then very great, yet was it subject to great alterations, by reason that he was a new Prince in his Dominions, because that they were far divided one from another, and for that many were apprehensive of so fast increasing greatness. So as many more

opportune and better grounded occasions might peradventure
arise of compassing such an intent, and the War made against
him by the Germans, which tended so much to his danger,
might prove such a one. By making fit use of which accidents,
Caesar's power might receive a rebuke as concerning the
affairs of Italy, if the French forces had some refuge, or that
the Italians had been of the same mind as formerly they had
been more unseasonably. Therefore to separate the friendship
of the French totally from the Italians, as Leo did for as much
as in him lay, discovering a double injury to them, since the
King of France might think that fraud was joined to ill will,
could not be but an ill-taken advice. He had done better to
have somewhat tempered their power as to the affairs of
Italy, than to have quite extinguished it, till the Italians
might get some better light how to recover their liberty.

The Venetian Senate took another course, though they
had therein the same intent: For whilst the affairs of these
two Princes, Charles the Emperor, and Francis King of France,
were in the greatest heat of War in Italy, they would apply
themselves to each of their fortunes, and according to the
condition of time and affairs, they often changed friendship;
being still constant in their aim, which was to keep their
Forces as equally balanced as they could, and that they
should both be weakened by their contention one with another:
But when occasion was offered of falling upon one without
too much advantage to the other, (as it did in the last Wars
made by the Venetians in Italy, after King Francis was let
out of Prison) they stood firm and resolute, not being easily
persuaded upon any conditions to lay down Arms. For on the
one side, Caesar's power did decline by reason of many adverse
changes, and the affairs of Naples were in great confusion and
danger: And on the other side, the affairs of France were not
much bettered as to the prejudice of the liberty of Italy; for a
chief Article in this Confederacy was, That the State of Milan
should be restored to Francesco Sforza, as at last it was. But
Leo in this conjuncture of affairs did precipitate himself into
friendship with the Imperialists, and drew the enmity of the
French upon him, so as his danger became almost equally the
same, whatever event the War should have; and the sequel

did all the more demonstrate this by the imprisonment of Clement, and by the slavery which Caesar's greatness threatened to all Italy.

So as it appears to reason, and by the sequel, that a noble and magnificent fabric, as Leo's proposition touching the freeing of Italy from the subjection of Foreigners was really to be esteemed, was not built upon so true and solid a foundation as was able to support so great a weight. But for the present, after many various accidents, the condition of affairs may be esteemed either good, or at least less bad; for as much as Italy, through Philip the King of Spain's great wisdom and moderation of mind, has enjoyed a long and peaceful condition, flourishes now as much as she has done in many preceding Ages, to the People's great comfort, and to the singular praise of the late Princes.

GIOVANNI BOTERO

OF THE COUNTERPOISE OF PRINCES' FORCES

[From: *Relatione della Republica Venetiana* (Venice 1605). pp. 8–11. Translated by John Warrington.]

Giovanni Botero (1544–1617) was an Italian prelate who, after a somewhat turbulent early career, rose to considerable eminence as a tutor and advisor in the employment of Archbishop Charles Borromeo of Milan, Cardinal Frederick Borromeo, and the Duke of Savoy. His best-known work, *Della ragion di Stato* (1589), contains little on the balance of power, but the essay published here for the first time in English has been largely neglected, mainly because of its obscure origins as a digression in his treatise *Relatione della Republica Venetiana* (1605). Its main contribution to the development of the balance-of-power idea is the central distinction between two types of counterpoise, although Lorenzo de' Medici might be more appropriately associated with the second than the first type.

Nature, who has so arranged that everything is balanced with antitheses and sustained by opposition, is seen to demonstrate clearly to princes both the necessity and 'the art of mutually counterpoising each other. If we look at the sky, we see the inestimable impetus of the Prime Mover with the contrary motion of the planets; the scorching heat of the Sun with the coldness of the Moon; the burning light of day tempered by the dewy darkness of night; the elements abated with opposite qualities; the year balanced with opposite seasons for the safety of mankind and the conservation of the universe. Nature, again, has given a short life to things that grow quickly, slow growth to those that last long; to wild plants natural fertility, and to cultivated ones man's artificial help. She has made large animals not very fertile, the tiny ones extremely fertile. She has given wild beasts an open and brave nature, a crafty and reserved one to those that are timid; she has endowed the former with a love of solitude, the latter with a craving for companionship. She has, in fact, left nothing without its counterpoise. What is braver than the lion? Yet it is frightened of the cock's crest and crow. What stronger than the elephant? Yet it trembles all over at the sight of a mouse. What vaster than the whale? Yet it needs the escort of a tiny fish. What faster than the dolphin? Yet its mouth is set far back, and for that reason it cannot easily catch its prey, though close at hand. The crocodile has its back protected by an impenetrable coat of scales; but because its belly is soft and delicate it is exposed to the dolphin's strike, which hunts it from below and disembowels it. *Intuere*, says Ecclesiasticus, *omnia opera altissimi: unum contra unum, duo contra duo; et non fecit quidpiam deesse*.[1] Likewise, to effect a balance in politics is simply to prevent others from disturbing the peace and endangering the security of states. Although Nature has made partial provision with mountains, lonely rivers, forests and arms of the sea, with differences of colour and customs, she has not been able so to act as to prevent the greed of ambitious men.

But before we go further, let us assume that where there is not a plurality of princes there can be no such balance as we are discussing, unless perhaps between parties and factions among the subject peoples. This is quite clear in Spain, England, France, Poland and other kingdoms, states at first divided into several principalities but subsequently united under a single crown. Now, if the whole world were under one republic or one prince, the art of counterpoise would be superfluous and quite unnecessary. Granted, however, a plurality of princes, it follows that a counterpoise is useful and good, not *per se* but *per accidem*. And it is of two kinds; for sometimes its purpose is the peace of a republic consisting of many different states, such as Italy, Germany, and Christendom as a whole, and at other times the security and well-being of one particular state. In the first case, the counterpoise consists in a certain levelling whereby the body of the republic has no members that are not proportioned among themselves and balanced with a certain equality: no part is of less weight than another.

In this respect Lorenzo de' Medici, Prince of the Florentine Republic, was once of great importance; for by keeping the less powerful Italian princes united he balanced the forces and checked the schemes of the more powerful, as a result of which Italy enjoyed a tranquil and happy peace in his day. This was later disturbed by his son Piero de' Medici, who, tightening his relationship with Ferdinand, King of Naples, alarmed Lodovico Sforza and caused him to invite the French into Italy. Thence proceeded the gravest calamities for Italy and Lodovico's own ruin. The popes, because of their supreme rank among Christians, have a large following with the party that seeks peace and the welfare of the Holy Church; glorious not with arms, which seldom achieve worthwhile results, but by the very high authority which the Pope, as common father, holds among Christian princes. Henry VIII, King of England, sought this by allying himself first with Charles V and then with Francis I, King of France, claiming to balance the affairs of Europe. And Henry (VII), his father, had wisely urged him above all else to maintain peace with the King of France, because only thus could the Kings of England reign in security and perfect felicity.

But this balance whose object is the security of one particular state concerns anyone who has dominion and wishes to secure it without having to depend on others. Ferdinand of Aragon, King of Spain, proved himself a very capable ruler:

by wonderfully skilful alliances, which he made or broke according to circumstances and his requirements, he not only kept together and secured his extensive dominions, but even managed to enlarge and greatly improve them.

Because the counterpoise is founded on this natural order and the light of reason (for just as it is lawful to repel force with force, it is equally lawful to provide against having to do so), it is reasonable, so long as others do not have to suffer, to oppose not only a suspect and openly hostile power but also a friendly and allied power which may one day turn out to be dangerous to oneself and one's own interests. Thus, Polybius tells us, Hiero, tyrant of Syracuse, although a respected friend of Rome, sent the Carthaginians valuable assistance, which they needed for purposes of a bloody war. For he feared that in the event of a Carthaginian defeat he might have to exchange the friendship of the Romans (to whose power no obstacle would remain) for servitude, and become their slave instead of an ally.

Just as those who, though able to profit by oppressing others, refrain from doing so, are rarer than white ravens, it is well known that although all desire that others' forces should be counterpoised, no one is willing that his own should be. Rome is an outstanding example. Unwilling that there should be in Italy a prince who might serve as a counterpoise to her own power, she refused to make a treaty of peace and accord with Pyrrhus, King of Epirus, unless he first left Italy. Again, in order to have no counterpoise in Europe, she deprived Philip of Macedon of part of his territory, and then stripped his son Perseus not only of his kingdom but also of his life. In order to have no counterpoise in Africa, she razed Carthage; in Asia, for the same reason, she drove Antiochus beyond the Taurus, and then waged unrelenting war against Mithridates until she drove him to suicide.

The ordinary method of counterpoising suspect forces that threaten one's own interests is the formation of leagues, whereby one force is set against another. To discuss such leagues in detail here would be altogether out of place. It need only be said that no trust should be placed in leagues that are not based on real interest and danger, or on equal utility to all parties; but more on the former rather than the latter. For we exert ourselves more effectively through fear of evil than through desire of good, and the reason is this: satisfied with present good, we can do without the good we desire; but we cannot prosper with evil close at hand.

[1] Botero has conflated two passages: Eccl. 33.15 ('And thus look upon all the works of the Most High; Two and two, one against another.'), and Eccl. 42.24 ('All things are double one against another: And he hath made nothing imperfect.'). *The Apocrypha, Revised Version* (Oxford, 1927).

The Early Seventeenth Century

ANONYMOUS

WHETHER IT BE EXPEDIENT TO MAKE PEACE WITH ENGLAND (*c.* 1600) *Extract*

[From: 'S'il est expedient de faire paix avec l'Angleterre'. *Papiers d'État et de l'Audience*, liasse 367, Archives Générales du Royaume de Belgique, Brussels. *By permission of the Archives Générales du Royaume de Belgique.* Translated by Dr Barbara Haines, University College of Wales.]

The views in this anonymous *mémoire* were presented to Archduke Albert of Austria, who held nominal sovereignty over the Spanish Netherlands with his wife Isabella, the daughter of Philip II of Spain. Written around 1600, the document presents arguments for and against ending the war with England which had dragged on after the defeat of the Armada in 1588. Since England was generally regarded as the head of the Protestant cause against which Philip II's Catholic Spain was such an ardent opponent, it is interesting that one of the principal arguments of the proponents of peace with England is the necessity to make a counterweight to France, whose power was said to be increasing, partly at the expense of the Spanish Netherlands. A number of other points are made for and against the proposed peace but they are not reproduced here. Peace was eventually concluded in 1604.

THE ARGUMENT IN FAVOUR

1. A peace that be reasonable, certain and assured, and not wrapped up in shame, dissimulation and deceit, is doubtless to be preferred to a perilous and uncertain war, being in accordance not only with the order and well-being of the state, but with the law of God and of Good Conscience.

2. Now it can be argued that this will be such a peace, that the certain fruits thereof will be of no small account. First, let us speak of Spain. The Indies fleet will be at liberty to sail the seas in greater surety, without harassment or travail, [this fleet] which constitutes the fibre, the strength of this kingdom

and all the others that depend upon it; the veins that do bring life to this great and vast body, and without which the means and revenues of Spain will always be uncertain and imperilled.

3. Upon conclusion of this peace, the English will straightway withdraw their men of war and no more molest these states [1] and Spanish shipping.

4. Spain's armadas will have free passage through the Narrow Seas and in their need, haven and shelter in the English ports, which is a very weighty consideration.

5. [This alliance] will be a salutary counter weight to the might and power of France, which nation, by virtue of the peace and order which her king maintains, will soon present a threat to daunt the princes of all Christendom—they being for the most part all engaged in war, while he enjoys a stable peace, founding his power on the ruination of these provinces,[1] principally, I do say, upon its manufactures which will all be moved to France, to the great and irreparable damage of these Provinces. For if France once breaks with Spain, and England be not her ally, then Spain will manifestly suffer, so that this must be one of the most pregnant considerations conspiring to unite these three states.[2] For the strongest bond in this alliance, *communis necessitas facit communes amicos*, and the same cause which joined France and England in alliance in these latest wars—which is to say the power of the King of Spain —must now unite Spain, England and this country.

6. This peace is thus expedient, and, as it were, necessary to Spain and therefore to this country which should not seek to dissolve its ties with Spain, for reasons of state of which all men are aware . . .

REJOINDER TO THIS ARGUMENT

A just and reasonable peace free of shame and dissimulation is doubtless to be preferred to a perilous and uncertain war. Yet in seeking to secure it, a man must never do an unjust or dishonourable deed, nor any evil thing however slight, in anticipation of the greater good. But a peace which is full of dissimulation, equivocation and deceit and—what be worse— full of unholiness and irreligion, is incomparably more perilous than all the divers and cruel wars that there may be. For beneath the name of peace there lurks a more treacherous state of war, and masquerading as a salutary balm there be a mortal poison.

There can be no assurance in that which depends solely on another's will and can be renegued to suit his own best interest. Weak indeed is that bond which rests solely on a promise. Nor will the Spanish fleet thereby escape harassment by the Dutchman's ships.[3]

To this point also [4] the same response is offered, that no assurance of good faith can likely issue from a fickle and a heretic princess,[5] defender of a contrary religion. That [Spain's fleets might have access to English ports] is no more certain than [that they will thereby be free from English attacks], and even were it certain, it would be of small account since we have the French ports that be open to our ships.

That [this peace will be a salutary counter weight to the power of France] must also be of little account. The might of France cannot be so great, not even were it joined to that of England, that that country could inspire the fear and terror of a monarch so puissant as the King of Spain, so long as he be able to order his affairs as should a wise and astute prince, and keep from plunging into civil and domestic strife in the very bosom of his lands, for this would be the death and utter ruin of his state. A foreign war, nay even one within his own realms and territories, could bring him but little harm for reasons that be very plain. And even were this peace agreed, there would be but little comfort and assurance in it seeing that England is the most deceitful and perfidious nation in the world, *infidi socii et iam hostes*, shifting with every changing wind—in witness whereof her conduct in the time of Charles V, our Emperor . . .

---

[1] Spanish Netherlands.
[2] England, Spain and the Spanish Netherlands.
[3] This is by way of rejoinder to the argument put forward earlier in 3.
[4] viz. Point 4 in the argument in favour of the peace.
[5] Queen Elizabeth I of England.

FRANCIS BACON

NOTES FOR A SPEECH CONCERNING A WAR WITH SPAIN (1623–1624)

[From: *The Letters and the Life of Francis Bacon*, vii. Ed. James Spedding, 1874. pp. 460–5.]

Francis Bacon (1561–1626), Lord Chancellor, philosopher and man of letters, drafted these 'Notes' for a Parliamentary speech to be made by someone else, and subsequently extended them in his well-known pamphlet, 'Considerations touching a War with Spain'. Although his analysis clearly subserves the advocacy of a specific course of action, Bacon's systematic assessment of the relative strengths of England and Spain, according to Experience and Reason, is closer to the original balancing metaphor than many subsequent writings. It is in the tradition of Botero's second type of counterpoise— that 'whose object is the security and well-being of a particular state' —and provides an early list of the elements of power which are to be weighed in the scales.

That ye conceive there will be little difference in opinion but that all will advise the King not to entertain further a treaty wherein he hath been so manifestly and so long deluded.

That the difficulty therefore will be in the consequences thereof. For to the breach of treaty doth necessarily succeed a despair of recovering the Palatinate by treaty: and so the business falleth upon a war. And to that you will apply your speech as being the point of importance and besides most agreeable to your profession and place.

To a war (such as may promise success) there are three things required: a just Quarrel; sufficient Forces and Provisions; and a prudent and politic choice of the Designs and Actions whereby the war shall be managed.

For the Quarrel. There cannot be a more just quarrel by the laws both of nature and nations than for the recovery of the ancient patrimony of the King's children gotten from them by an usurping sword and an insidious treaty.

But further, that the war well considered is not for the Palatinate only but for England and Scotland. For if we stay till the Low-Countrymen be ruined and the party of the papists within the realm be grown too strong, England, Scotland and Ireland are at the stake.

Neither doth it concern the State only but our Church. Other kings, papists content themselves to maintain their religion in their own dominions. But the kings of Spain run a course to make themselves protectors of the popish religion even amongst the subjects of other kings. Almost like the Ottomans that profess to plant the law of Mahomet by the sword; and so the Spaniards do of the Pope's law. And therefore if either the King's blood or our own blood or Christ's blood be dear unto us, the quarrel is just, and to be embraced.

For the point of sufficient Forces. The balancing of the forces of these kingdoms and their allies with Spain and their allies you know to be a matter of great and weighty considera-tion. But yet to weigh them in a common understanding, for your part you are of opinion that Spain is no such giant; or if he be a giant, it will be but like Goliath and David; for God will be on our side.

But to leave these spiritual considerations, you do not see in true discourse of State and War that we ought to doubt to be overmatched. To this opinion you are led by two things which lead all men; by Experience and by Reason.

For Experience. You do not find that for this age (take it for one hundred years), there was ever any encounter between Spanish and English of importance either by sea or land but the English came off with the honour; witness the Lammas day, the retreat of Gaunt, the battle of Newport, and some others. But there have been some actions both by sea and land so memorable as scarce suffer the less to be spoken of. By sea, that of eighty-eight, when the Spaniards putting them-selves most upon their stirrups sent forth that invincible Armada which should have swallowed up England quick. The success whereof was, that although that fleet swam like mountains upon our seas yet they did not so much as take a cock-boat of ours at sea nor fire a cottage at land, but came through our channel and were driven as Sir Walter Raleigh says by squibs (fire-boats he means) from Calais, and were soundly beaten by our ships in fight, and many of them sunk, and finally durst

not return the way they came, but made a scattered perambu-
lation full of shipwracks by the Irish and Scottish seas to get
home again; just according to the curse of the Scripture, that
they came out against us one way and fled before us seven
ways. By land, who can forget the two voyages made upon the
continent itself of Spain; that of Lisbon and that of Cales.
When in the former we knocked at the gates of the greatest
city either of Spain or Portugal and came off without seeing
an enemy to look upon us in the face. And though we failed in
our foundation (for that Antonio whom we thought to replace
in his kingdom found no party at all); yet it was a true trial of
the gentleness of Spain, which suffered us to go and come
without any dispute. And for the latter, of Cales, it ended in
victory; we ravished a principal city of wealth and strength
in the high countries, sacked it, fired the Indian fleet that was
in the port, and came home in triumph; and yet to this day
were never put in suit for it, nor demanded reason for our
doings. You ought not to forget the battle of Kinsale in Ireland,
what time the Spanish forces were joined with the Irish (good
soldiers as themselves or better) and exceeded us far in number,
and yet they were soon defeated, and their general D'Avila
taken prisoner, and that war by that battle quenched and ended.

And it is worthy to be noted how much our power in those
days was inferior to our present state. Then; a lady; old; and
owner only of England; intangled with the revolt of Ireland,
and her confederates of Holland much weaker and in no conjuncture. Now; a famous King and strengthened with a
Prince of singular expectation, and in the prime of his years;
owner of the entire isle of Britain; enjoying Ireland populate
and quiet, and infinitely more supported by confederates of
the Low Countries, Denmark, divers of the princes of Germany,
and others. As for the comparison of Spain as it was then and
as it is now you will for good respects forbear to speak. Only
you will say this, That Spain was then reputed to have the
wisest counsel of Europe, and not a counsel that would come
at the whistle of a favourite.

Another point of experience you would not speak of, if it
were not that there is a wonderful erroneous observation
walketh about contrary to all the true account of time; and it

is, That the Spaniard where he once gets in will seldom or never be got out again (and they give it an ill-favoured simile which you will not name). But nothing is less true. They got footing at Brest and some other parts in Britaine, and quitted it. They had Calais, Ardes, Amiens, and were part beaten out and part they rendered. They had Vercelles in Savoy, and fairly left it. They had the other day the Valtoline, and now have put it in deposit. What they will do at Ormus we shall see. So that, to speak truly, of later times they have rather poached and offered at a number of enterprises than maintained any constantly. And for Germany in more ancient time, their great emperor Charles after he had Germany almost in his fist was forced in the end to go from Isburgh as it were in a mask by torch-light and to quit every foot of his new acquests in Germany: which you hope likewise will be the hereditary issue of this late purchase of the Palatinate. And thus much for Experience.

For Reason. It hath many branches; you will but extract a few.

First; It is a nation thin sown of men, partly by reason of the sterility of their soil; and partly because their natives are exhaust by so many employments in such vast territories as they possess. So that it hath been counted a kind of miracle to see together ten or twelve thousand native Spaniards in an army. And although they have at this time great numbers of miscellany soldiers in their armies and garrisons, yet if there should be the misfortune of a battle they are ever long about it to draw on supplies. They tell a tale of a Spanish ambassador that was brought to see the treasury of St Mark at Venice, and still he looked down to the ground; and being asked the reason, said he was looking to see whether the treasure had any root, so that if that were spent it would grow again, as his master's had. But howsoever it be of their treasure, certainly their forces have scarcely any root, or at least such a root as putteth forth very poorly and slowly; whereas there is not in the world again such a spring and seminary of military people as is England, Scotland and Ireland; nor of seamen as is this island and the Low Countries. So as if the wars should mow them down, yet they suddenly may be supplied and come up again.

A second reason is (and it is the principal) that if we truly consider the greatness of Spain it consisteth chiefly in their treasure, and their treasure in their Indies and their Indies (both of them) is but an accession to such as are masters by sea. So as this axle-tree whereupon their greatness turns is soon cut a-two by any that shall be stronger than they at sea. So then you report yourself to their opinions, and the opinions of all men, enemies or whosoever; whether that the maritime forces of Britain and the Low Countries are not able to beat them at sea. For if that be, you see the chain is broken, from shipping to Indies, from Indies to treasure, and from treasure to greatness.

The third reason (which hath some affinity with this second) is a point comfortable to hear in the state that we now are. Wars are generally causes of poverty and consumption. The nature of this war, you are persuaded, will be matter of restorative and enriching. So that, if we go roundly on with supplies and provisions at the first, the war in continuance will find itself. That you do but point at this and will not enlarge it.

Lastly, That it is not a little to be considered that the greatness of Spain is not only distracted extremely and therefore of less force; but built upon no very sound foundations; and therefore they can have the less strength by any assured and confident confederates. With France they are in competition for Navarre, Milan, Naples, and the Franche County of Burgundy. With the see of Rome, for Naples also. For Portugal, with the right heirs of that line. For that they have in their Low Countries, with the United Provinces. For Ormus (now) with Persia. For Valencia with the Moors expulsed and their confederates. For the East and West Indies with all the world. So that if every bird had his feather Spain would be left wonderful naked. But yet there is a greater confederation against them than by means of any of these quarrels or titles; and that is contracted by the fear that almost all nations have of their ambition, whereof men see no end. And thus much for the balancing of their Forces.

For the last point, which is the choice of the Designs and Enterprises, in which to conduct the war, you will not now speak. Because you should be forced to descend to divers particulars whereof some are of a more open and some of a

more secret nature. But that you would move the House to
make a selected committee for that purpose. Not to estrange
the House in any sort but to prepare things for them, giving
them power and commission to call before them and to confer
with any martial men or others that are not of the House that
they shall think fit, for their advice and information. And so to
give an account of the business to a general committee of the
whole House.

PHILIPPE DE BÉTHUNE

OF TREATIES OF NEUTRALITY (1632)

[From: *The Counsellor of Estate*. Translated by E. G., 1634. pp. 217–20.]

Philippe de Béthune (1561–1649) was considered by his contemporaries to be one of the outstanding diplomats of his era; he success-
fully completed several difficult missions in the service of Henry IV
and Louis XIII, often in a mediatory role. His major work, *Le
Conseiller d'estat*, was written in retirement and published in several
editions, including a contemporary English translation. His discussion
of the balance of power in the chapter on neutrality owes something
to Bodin's *Six Livres de la République*, but his distinction between
absolute and conditional power breaks new ground.

Let us come to Treaties of Neutrality, the which seems
natural to Princes, who neither love nor hate anything absolutely; but govern themselves in their Friendships according
to their interests. And in effect Reason of State is no other
thing but Reason of interest.

Neutrality may be of two sorts. The one with Alliance with
both sides: The other without Alliance, and without any tie
to the one or the other; which is that, that may properly be
called Neutrality. The first has Rules prescribed by the conditions of the Treaty. The second has no Rule, but the discretion
of the neuter Prince, who must carry himself in such sort, as
he may not make show that he inclines more to one side than
to another. And for that the Affairs of Princes are not always

in one Estate, the Difficulty is to know when the Prince should leave this Neutrality, and when he should maintain it.

The advantages of Neutrality are, that he which is Neuter, is honoured and respected of both parties, for the fear that either of them has, should he declare himself against him: He remains Arbitrator of others and Master of himself; He enjoys the present, and according to occasions takes advantage of the future. A Neuter is without any professed Enemy, and offends or wrongs no man openly; so that, where there is no involvement, one is troubled to find a pretext to do him harm.

The disadvantages are, that a Neuter satisfies neither the one nor the other; and so remains: He does neither purchase Friends, nor free himself from any Enemies; and in the end is made a prey to the Victor. And many have held it more advantageous to hazard themselves to vanquish with a companion, than to remain in an Estate, where there is an assurance of ruin by the one or the other.

To resolve this point, a powerful Prince has no need of Counsel. For in what fashion soever he remains, he may maintain himself, and prescribe a Law to others. Yet I hold that without great occasion he should not declare himself. For that whilst others ruin themselves by war, he fortifies himself with means; he may in the end make himself Judge of their differences, and settling them gently with honour, he preserves their Friendship and maintains his Estate.

But in a weak Prince, what part soever he takes, it will be hurtful unto him; especially if he be in the midst of two more powerful Estates than himself. Yet I will say, that speaking generally, a Neutrality is more beneficial to a weak Prince, provided that they which make War one against the other, be not altogether barbarous and inhuman. For although a Neutrality does not please either party; yet in effect it wrongs no man; and as he which is a Neuter, does not serve, so he does not hurt. And then, since the outcome of the Declaration made for the one rather than the other, depends upon the uncertain issue of the War, he should have no cause to say, that this course is more safe than a Neutrality. And to change his resolution without an assurance of bettering his affairs, were not to carry himself wisely.

But if the Neuter be pressed by necessity to declare himself, he must do it for the most powerful of the two parties, following the Counsel of that *Roman*: that either one must make oneself the strongest, or be a friend to the strongest; unless he sees that joining with the weakest, he might balance the power of the strongest, and by this counterpoise reduce them to reason. The safety of Estates consisting chiefly in an equal counterpoise of power on both sides, and the greatness of a Prince drawing after it the ruin of his Neighbours; it is wisdom to prevent this.

But power is considered in this subject diversely: Either absolute or conditional; Absolute power is that which we measure by the concurrence of the greatness of Forces, Treasure, Munitions, and other Military preparations. Conditional power is that, the which although it be less than absolute power, yet it is more fit to succour us, or to do us harm. In this Neighbourhood is of very great consideration; for that a Neighbour Prince of mean forces, may more easily or sooner hurt or succour us, than a great Prince which lies far off. Near succours are always sooner ready and with less charge: For we may dismiss a part of it when time and occasion shall serve: If he be remote, he arrives too late after the occasion to defend us, and soon enough to oppress us. The greatest part perishes on the way; and when he has arrived he has more need to rest than to fight; and being unable to send him back so far, we must still bear the charge and oppression.

Hiero King of *Syracuse*, could well observe these considerations, the *Carthaginians* being Masters of a part of *Sicily*, he allied himself with them against the *Romans*: But the *Romans* having become the strongest in the country, he fell to their side, and continued the War with them against the *Carthaginians*, who were then more remote from the Island than the *Romans*.

After we have made consideration of the force, we must likewise consider of the courage and constancy of the Prince, with whom we are to join. For if he be light and has no stay, how powerful soever he be, it is dangerous to be engaged with him: But if with these advantages he knows how to prosecute his designs with resolution, one may boldly engage oneself with him.

DUKE HENRI DE ROHAN

[From: *A Treatise of the Interest of the Princes and States of Christendome.* Translated into English by H. H. Paris 1640. pp. 1–3, 18–21, 24–5.]

The Duke of Rohan (1579–1638), Huguenot general and statesman, distinguished himself in the service of Henry IV, after whose death he became the leader of the Huguenots in the religious wars. He was exiled to Venice where he became a 'generalissimo', but later regained Richelieu's confidence serving briefly as Ambassador in Switzerland in 1632. His most famous work, *De l'interest des Princes et Estats de la Chrestienté*, was published in 1638 and appeared in a widely read English translation two years later. This treatise, although coloured by Rohan's anti-Spanish bias, is the first systematic linking of the notions of balance and interest. The first part is a country-by-country survey, of which the preface and the chapters on Italy and Savoy are reproduced here, while the second part consists of seven discourses on recent history.

THE PREFACE

The Princes command the People, and the Interest commands the Princes. The knowledge of this Interest is as much more raised above that of princes' actions, as they themselves are above the People. The Prince may deceive himself, his Counsel may be corrupted, but the interest alone can never fail. According as it is well or ill understood, it causes States to live or die. And as it always aims at the augmentation, or at least the conservation of a State, so likewise to get thither, it ought to vary according to the times. So that to consider well the interest of the Princes of this time, we need not remount very far, but only take the standing of the present affairs. For this purpose one ought to lay for a ground, that there be two Powers in Christendom, which are as the two Poles, from whence descend the influences of peace and war upon the other states, to wit, the houses of France and Spain. That of Spain finding herself augmented all at once, has not been able to conceal the design she had to make herself Mistress, and cause the Sun of a new Monarchy to rise in the West. That of France is forthwith carried to make a counter-

poise. The other Princes join the one or the other, according
to their interest. But for as much as this interest (as it had been
well or ill followed) has caused the ruin of some, or the greatness
of others, I have purposed to publish in this present Treatise:
First what was the true interest of these two mighty Powers,
and then of the others which seem in some manner to depend
on their protection. Next of all I shall show how much has
been the digression from this true interest, either because it
was not well understood by the Prince or else because it was
concealed from him by the corruption of his Ministers. . . .

OF THE INTEREST OF THE PRINCES OF ITALY

Italy, which is environed with the Alps and the Mediter-
ranean Sea, after the deluge of those Barbary nations that so
long time afflicted it, seemed as if she ought to think of nothing
more than to profit from the opportunity of her situation, to
keep herself close and secret, being as well separated by the
interest of her Provinces, as she was divided by her position.
And truly it was then the maxim which they should have
followed; for these little Princes could live peaceably under the
shadow of the greater, which having amongst themselves their
just counterpoise, could not attempt any thing upon their
inferiors. And the principal Powers sharing amongst themselves the dominion of such a Country, had reason to exclude
their neighbours from the Knowledge of their affairs.

But since that the King of Spain has set foot in Italy, and
that finding himself Master of both ends thereof, he has made
the balance incline on his own side, the true interest in general
of the Italian Princes has been to keep ever at least one gate
open, to guard themselves from the oppression which such a
formidable Power might make them fear.

And although that for this effect they ought to hold intelli-
gences with other Princes, it behoves them notwithstanding,
to do it chiefly with the King of France, for three reasons.
First, for the nearness, and opportunity of being able to
succour them, either by sea or land. Secondly, for the great
forces that this great Realm can set on foot. And lastly, by
this bridle to restrain the Spaniard, who otherwise would
carry himself towards them with less moderation.

The other maxim which Italy ought to observe is to conserve herself in peace. First, because there can be no war, but the Kings of France and Spain will there take part, either as favouring one of the parties, or else as Arbitrators. Besides it ought to be considered, that war cannot be enkindled in this Country, without great danger of stirring up diverse humours, which do now lie still.

These are the two points wherein lies the interest of Italy in general. And although that every Prince ought to have the same aim, there are notwithstanding certain particular interests in each State. The Commonwealth of Venice in regard of the extent of her dominion both by sea and land, likewise of the firmness of her establishment for twelve centuries entire, and of the prudent conduct of so wise a government, is without doubt the chief Power of Italy next that of the King of Spain, and she also has been the first Commonwealth that has settled the rules of her conservation, and that has most punctually observed them, in taking for her particular interest, that of Italy in general. Moreover for particular respects she makes it a maxim, to hold a straight intelligence with the Turk, and for the same she spares not any cost. She believes also that her interest is, to maintain war abroad and foment the same with money. That which the other Princes of Italy ought also to do, if they had strength and courage to undertake it.

She loses no time for to hinder the King of Spain and the Pope from waxing great. The State of Venice seems extraordinarily jealous of these two Potentates, though it be a maxim common to all Princes to hinder the growth of their Neighbours. As for the other Princes of Italy she upholds them according to her own benefit. . . .

OF THE INTEREST OF THE DUKE OF SAVOY

It remains only for conclusion, to speak of the Duke of Savoy. The Estate of this Prince is in such manner situated, that to which side soever he turns, he can bring great weight to the party he embraces. Charles Emanuel (who was first willing to make known that a Duke of Savoy could make peace and war in Italy) believed, that the interest of his Estate was, to side one while with France, another while with Spain, according to the occurrences and good of his affairs, which was the sole aim of his designs, without thinking of Treaties made either with the one or the other. But this Prince, full of vast thoughts, and who could not bound his ambition by the barriers that Nature has set to his Estate, was glad that the situation of his Country might serve for a pretext to his disquiet.

For indeed the true interest of a Duke of Savoy is, to have always a good correspondence with France, because she can assist him with the whole mass of her forces, against one member of the power of Spain,[1] who has more jealousy of her Estates in Italy, than (to say in a manner) of all the rest together, who has a vehement desire to join Piedmont to the Duchy of Milan. So as, the Duke of Savoy should believe, that what amity soever he has with Spain, it is most dangerous to him. He ought nevertheless to entertain it, in so much as it is needful to guard him from France.

[1] viz. Milan.

The Age of Louis XIV

FRANÇOIS DE SALIGNAC DE LA MOTHE FÉNELON

ON THE NECESSITY OF FORMING ALLIANCES, BOTH OFFENSIVE AND DEFENSIVE, AGAINST A FOREIGN POWER WHICH MANIFESTLY ASPIRES TO UNIVERSAL MONARCHY (*c.* 1700)

[From: 'Two Essays on the Balance of Europe . . . Printed in the Year 1720'. *A Collection of Scarce and Valuable Tracts* (*Lord Somers Tracts*), xiii. 2nd edition, 1815. pp. 766–70. (Material added by the eighteenth-century translator, William Grant, has been removed.)]

François de Salignac de la Mothe Fénelon (1651–1715) was a French prelate who became Archbishop of Cambrai in 1695 but then fell out of favour with Louis XIV as a result of a religious controversy. Exiled to his diocese, he wrote a number of works, including *L'Examen de conscience sur les devoirs de la royauté* (1700), which was intended for the education of the young Duke of Burgundy, a possible successor to Louis XIV. The *Supplément* printed here contains probably the best-known justification of the balance of power on natural law principles and includes an analysis of '*quatre sortes de systèmes*'.

Neighbouring states are not only obliged to observe towards each other the rules of justice and public faith; but they are under a necessity, for the security of each, and the common interest of all, to maintain together a kind of society and general republic; for the most powerful will certainly at length prevail and overthrow the rest, unless they unite together to make a counterweight.

It is not to be expected, among men, that a superior power will contain itself within the bounds of an exact moderation, and that it will not employ its force to obtain for itself what advantages it can, by oppressing the weaker. Or if this power should happen to be for some time harmless in the hands of an excellent prince, who could bear such prosperity so well, the wonder, 'tis likely, would cease with his reign: For the natural ambition of princes, the flatteries of their courtiers, and the prejudices of nations themselves will not suffer us to believe that a people who had it in their power to subdue their neighbours, would abstain from it for any considerable time. A reign conspicuous for such extraordinary justice, would be the ornament of history, and a prodigy not to be looked for again.

We are then to expect, what in reality we see frequently happen, that every nation will seek to prevail over its neighbours; and therefore every nation is obliged, for its proper security, to watch against, and by all means restrain the excessive increase of greatness in any of its neighbours. Nor is this injustice; 'tis to preserve itself and its neighbours from servitude; 'tis to contend for the liberty, tranquillity, and happiness of all in general: For the over-increase of power in any one influences the general system of all the surrounding nations. Thus the successive changes which have happened in the house of Burgundy, and which afterwards raised that of Austria, have altered the face of affairs throughout Europe. All Europe had reason to dread an universal monarchy under Charles V, especially after he had defeated and taken Francis I at Pavia. 'Tis certain that a nation, having no pretence directly to meddle with the affairs of Spain, had at that time a very good right to oppose that formidable power which appeared ready to swallow up all.

Private men indeed have no right to oppose the increase of their neighbour's wealth, because they cannot pretend it may prove prejudicial or destructive to them. There are laws and magistrates to suppress injustice and violence among families unequal in power.

But the case of states is different, the overgrowth of one of these may prove the ruin and enslavement of all its neighbours. Here are neither laws nor judges established for a barrier against the invasions of the strongest; they have, therefore, reason to suppose that the strongest will invade their liberties as soon as there is no force sufficient to oppose them. Each of them may and ought to prevent that increase of power which would endanger the liberty of his own people, and that of all his neighbours. For example, Philip II of Spain, after he had conquered Portugal, would have made himself master of

England. 'Tis true, he had no right that was well founded; but supposing his right to have been incontestable, it was the interest of all Europe to oppose his establishment in England; because so powerful a kingdom, added to his other dominions of Spain, Italy, Flanders, and the Indies, would have enabled him to subject by his maritime force all the other powers of Christendom. Then *summum jus, summa injuria.*[1] Any particular right of succession or donation, should have given way to the natural law that provides for the security of so many nations. Whatever destroys the balance and tends to set up an universal monarchy, can be no other than unjust; however it may be founded on the written laws of a particular country, which can never prevail over the sovereign and universal law of nature for the common security and liberty, engraven in the hearts of all the nations of the world.

When a power is grown to such a pitch that all its neighbours are hardly a match for it, they have an undoubted right to unite for the restraining of that increase, which, were it suffered to proceed, would become too great to be opposed in its attempts on the common liberty. But that such confederacies for restraining the growing power of a state may be lawful, the danger from it must be real and pressing; the league defensive, or no further offensive than a just and necessary defence requires; and such bounds must be set to it as it may not entirely destroy that power which it was formed only to limit and moderate.

This care to maintain a kind of equality and balance among neighbouring nations, is that which secures the common repose; and in this respect such nations, being joined together by commerce, compose, as it were one great body and a kind of community. Christendom, for example, makes a sort of general republic which has its interests, its dangers, and its policy. All the members of this great body owe to one another for the common good, and to themselves for their particular security, that they oppose the progress of any one member, which may destroy the balance, and tend to the inevitable ruin of the other members. Whatever alters the general system of Europe is dangerous, and draws after it many fatal consequences.

All neighbouring nations are so connected together by their
mutual interests, that the least progress of any one is sufficient
to alter the general balance, which makes the security of the
whole; as when one stone is taken out of an arch, the whole
falls to the ground, because all the stones sustain each other
in pushing against each other. 'Tis a duty then for neighbouring
nations to concur for the common safety against one who
grows too powerful, as it is for fellow-citizens to unite against
an invader of the liberty of their country. If there is a duty
owing by every citizen to his particular society or country,
every nation, by the same reason, is obliged to consult the
welfare and repose of that universal republic of which it is a
member and in which are enclosed all the countries composed
of private men.

These defensive alliances are then just and necessary, when
they are in reality intended to prevent an exorbitant power,
such as might be in a condition to subdue all. Nor can the
superior power justly break the peace with the lesser states,
merely upon account of their defensive leagues, which it was
their right and their duty to enter into. The justice of these
leagues depends on their circumstances: They should be
founded on some infractions of the peace, or the seizure of
some places of the allies, or some certain ground of the like
nature: They ought likewise to be limited by such conditions
as may prevent (what we have often seen) one nation's pre-
tending a necessity of reducing another which aspires to universal tyranny, only that itself may succeed in the same design.

The address, as well as justice and faith required in making
treaties of alliance, is to frame them as plain as possible, and
as remote from an equivocal meaning, and exactly calculated
for procuring a certain benefit which you would immediately
be possessed of. You must take care that the engagements you
lay yourself under, do not reduce your enemy too low, and
prove too beneficial to your ally; which may lay you under a
necessity either to suffer what may be ruinous to you, or to
violate your engagements. And of these, 'tis hard to determine
which is more fatal.

Let us proceed to reason upon these principles, applying
them to Christendom, in which we are most interested.

There are only four cases, or conditions, in which a state may be supposed to be, with respect to its share of power in Europe.

The first is, when it has a force absolutely superior to that of all the other powers even united : Such was that of the Romans, and that of Charlemagne.

The second is, when it has a force superior to the rest, who nevertheless, uniting together, make a counterpoise to it.

The third is, when it has a force inferior to another, but supports itself by an union with the rest of its neighbours against the predominant power.

Lastly, the fourth is, when it has a force nearly equal to that of another neighbouring state, together with which it maintains all in peace, by a kind of balance which it preserves without ambition and with good faith.

The state of the Romans and of Charlemagne is by no means a desirable condition. First, because to arrive at it, you must commit all manner of injustice and violence; seize what is not your own, and that by the most bloody and continued wars. Then the design is very dangerous : States have often perished by these ambitious follies. And lastly, vast empires, which have been formed by means of so many mischiefs, are generally the occasion of others yet more dreadful by their fall. The first minority, or weak reign, dissolves the over-grown body, and separates the people, yet unaccustomed to the yoke of subjection, or to mutual union. Then what divisions, what confusions, what anarchies, without remedy! To be sensible of this, we need only reflect on the mischiefs brought on the west, by the sudden downfall of the empire of Charlemagne; and on the east, by the subversion of that of Alexander, whose captains made greater havoc in sharing the spoils of his victory, than he had done in the conquest of Asia. This then is of all the cases the most dazzling and fallacious, and the most fatal in its consequences to those who arrive at it.

The second case is that of a power superior to any one of the rest, who altogether make a balance against it. The advantage lies on the side of the superior power, in that it is united, simple, not subject to control, uniform and certain in its measures. But if it be not able to disunite the rest, by exciting jealousies among them, it must at length be overpowered, and all its superior force dwindle away; 'tis exposed to so many unlooked-for accidents within itself, or to be suddenly overthrown by invasions from abroad. Then it exerts itself to no purpose in destructive efforts for a superiority, which can afford it no real advantage, and which exposes it to all manner of disgraces and dangers. This is certainly the most wretched state of all, especially because even the most astonishing prosperity can only result in its passing into the first condition which we have already found to be unjust and pernicious.

The third case is that of a power inferior to another, which yet being united to the rest of Europe, makes a balance against the superior, and becomes the security of all the lesser states. This condition has its inconveniences, but it is less hazardous than the former; because 'tis on the defensive, it wastes itself less, it has its allies, and is generally in that state of inferiority, void of the blind inconsiderate presumption which is incident to the fortunate, and so often brings on the fall of the most prosperous states. Provided the inferior state be discreet and moderate, firm to its allies, and cautious not to give them the least ground of mistrust, nor to do any thing but in concert with them, and for the common good, it will be able to contend with the superior power, and at length reduce it.

The fourth case is that of a power equal to another, with which it maintains the balance, through a regard to the public security. This condition, without any ambitious attempts to alter it, is the wisest and happiest of all: You are the common arbiter; all your neighbours are your friends; or such as are not so, are therefore suspected by the rest: You do nothing which does not appear to have been intended for the good of your neighbours as well as of your own people: You add daily to your own strength; and when at length you come, as you cannot fail by a wise government to do, to have more force at home, and more alliances abroad than the power which is jealous of yours, then you must establish more and more that prudent moderation with which you have ever maintained the balance and the common security, and be ever mindful of the mischiefs which are caused by great conquests in the conquering state itself, as well as outside it; of their fruitlessness; of the danger of attempting them; finally of the vanity, uselessness and short duration of great empires and of the calamities which attend their fall.

But as it is not to be expected that a power superior to all others can long maintain itself at that height without abusing its superiority, it would become a wise and just prince not to wish to leave to his successors, who probably will not be so moderate as himself, the continual and violent temptation of a too pronounced superiority. For the good, therefore, of his successors and his people, he ought to confine himself to some equality with his neighbours.

'Tis true, there are two kinds of superiority: One is external, and consists in extent of territories, the number of fortified places, and the possession of passes into the neighbouring countries, etc. This proves a temptation to enterprises as fatal to the possessor of it, as to his neighbours; and excites against him hatreds, jealousies, and confederacies.

The other kind of superiority is inward and substantial; it consists in a more numerous people, better disciplined, and more skilful in agriculture and other necessary arts. This kind of superiority is generally the easiest attained, the surest, the least exposed to the envy and combinations of its inferior neighbours, and more proper than numerous conquests, and fortified places, to render a people invincible. A state cannot too diligently aspire to this superiority, nor too carefully avoid the former, which has no other than a false lustre.

[1] 'More law, more injustice' (Cicero, *De Officiis* I. 33).

DANIEL DEFOE

[From: *A Review of the State of the English Nation*, iii, no. 65 (really 66). 1st June 1706. pp. 261–3.]

Daniel Defoe (1660–1731), though better known for his fiction, is described by his biographer, James Sutherland, as 'one of the great English masters' for his controversial and journalistic writings. He was a pamphleteer in the service of successive ministries, both Tory and Whig, until shortly before his death, and his *Review* was a main

government organ from 1704 until 1713. He was a staunch supporter
of William of Orange, whose statecraft perfectly exemplified for
Defoe the principle of the balance of power. Although the balance of
power was something 'we have made much ado about in the World'
(*Review*, 23rd Sept. 1704), Defoe complained that it is 'little understood' (*Review*, 19th April 1709). To the task of correcting this state
of affairs he devoted many pages of the *Review*, usually in connection
with the War of the Spanish Succession, as in this case.

In my Enquiries and Suggestions, of what may or may not
be the Consequences of the great and glorious Successes of the
Confederate Forces against the French; one Word, like an
Echo, haunts me every Step I take, *viz.* WHAT'S NEXT?
Thus when *Antwerp*, *Ghent* and *Bruges*, etc. any thing else, our
Imagination makes reasonable, shall fall, *What's next*, or
what then? why then march into *Picardy*, says the last Paper but
one,[1] and still *what then* follows the Prescription, the inquisitive
Nature of Man leading him upon repeated Enquiries in every
thing.

Life itself is a Progression of Inquiry, a continued search
after something new, something more; and, WHAT'S NEXT,
runs thro' all the Actions of Men, till they come to a full stop
at the Grave; and then the grand Eclarcissment, or the full
Discovery of all that's subsequent, is made at once, and the
Enquiry ceases.

Now, that if possible, I may bring this progressive Motion,
or Line of Question to a full Stop, to a Period, and set a bound
at least to what we ought to enquire, if not, to what we will
enquire; I shall suggest now more Questions, and more than
any wise man will think tolerable, much less probable, and
yet amongst the greatest Crowd of our Wishes bring all to a
full Stop.

I brought the *English* Army in our last Enquiry,[2] where I
heartily wish I could see them, *viz.* in the very Bowels of
France, carving out large Conquests there, and no Enemy to
oppose them; the *Dutch* Army left behind, keeping the *French*
Troops that are remaining, at a constant Bay unable to help
themselves.

Well, Gentlemen, and WHAT NEXT? Why then the Duke
may traverse *Picardy*, ravage the Country, raise Contributions,

take all their Sea coast, and march up to the Gates of *Roan*, ay, and *Paris* too, say some; tho' perhaps they don't so well know what they talk of, *as they think they do*; but suppose for once, they had *Dunkirk*, *Calais*, *Boulogne*, and all the Sea Towns, and *what next*? Why, then suppose *France* harrassed, invaded in several Places from *Languedoc*, from *Spain*, from the Sea, or *where you will*, in as many places as you can, and *what next*? Suppose, the *French* King under the worst and most desperate Circumstances anybody can make rational, *what's next*? And here I shall differ from you all Gentlemen, and I cannot help it, my *next*, and *your next* will differ.

When all these things are brought to pass, ay, or half of them; of which I should be very glad,—and if any Man ask me then *what's next*, my Answer would be PEACE; and because I am *even more than any body* obliged to explain my self in every thing: I say, I desire to enter a little into the Meaning of what I say, and the Reasons of it; and when I have done that, you are welcome to pass your Censures.

I make no doubt, that *this is* a most just War begun upon the best Foundations; and perhaps the only just Foundations of a War, *viz. Peace*; 'tis a War for *Peace* and *Liberty*; all the pretensions Declarations and Claims of the Confederacy are to reduce *not France*, but the *exorbitant Power of France*; all the professed Intention of the Nation in this War, is to restore a lasting Peace to *Europe*, and bring *France* to Reason: Nor indeed, can any thing else be a due Foundation of War, the Blood of the many thousands of People, that fall in the public Quarrels of Princes, can no other way be accounted for but Defence of native and just Right, and preserving the public Peace and Good of the Country.

> War dies of Course, when e're Oppressions **cease**;
> They only justly fight, that fight for Peace.

Nor am I without a Voucher for my Opinion, and that from no less an Authority than him, who is *the likeliest Man in the World to bring it to pass*; I mean his Grace the Duke of *Marlborough*. If we look into the Duke's letter from *Flanders* to Mr Secretary *Harley*, we shall there find, the utmost Designs of that Glorious Prince are bounded by this very thing, as the

highest Advantage which can be obtained for this Nation.—
*I pray God continue the success of her Majesty's Arms, says the Duke,
till the Enemy may be brought to the Necessity of accepting a firm and
SOLID PEACE.*

'Tis evident, this is her Majesty's Design; 'tis evident, 'tis
the Duke of *Marlborough's* Aim; 'tis evident, 'tis the General
Interest, and any thing beyond it would be the Ruin and
Destruction both of us and the whole Confederacy, by break-
ing one way or other the Balance, which to obtain, is the End
and real Life of the present Conjunction of Powers in
Europe.

Whoever they are that wish this War to end in any thing
but a firm and solid peace, have either little to lose, get Money
by, or depend upon the War, or do not understand the Interest
and true Benefit of their native Country.

We do not fight for Conquest, but for Peace; 'tis *Peace* only can
restore the Breaches War has made upon our Commerce;
Peace only can make our Wealth flow like a high Spring Tide.
Indeed there are Circumstances by which we must say, we
shall *thrive with the War*, and of which I shall speak by itself;
but 'tis a Sort of thriving we ought not to court, in Competition
with a settled Conclusion of the War; nor can it be compared
to the Prosperity and Increase, which the Advantages of Trade,
opened and settled by Peace, must bring to such a Trading
Nation as this.

The End of this War is to reduce exorbitant Power to a due
Pitch, to run it quite down, would be to erect some *other
Exorbitant* in its Room; and so set up ourselves as public
Enemies to *Europe*, in the Room of that public Enemy we pull
down.

Every Power, which over balances the rest, *makes itself a
Nuisance* to its Neighbours. *Europe* being divided into a great
Variety of separate Governments and Constitutions; the
Safety of the whole consists in a due Distribution of Power, so
shared to every Part or Branch of Government, that no one
may be able to oppress and destroy the rest.

And 'tis evident from Experience, that whenever it has been
otherwise, the Consequence has been, potent Confederacies
among the weaker Powers by Joint Assistance to reduce the

encroaching growing Part to such Terms of Reason, and preserve and secure the Tranquillity of the rest.

When that Power is reduced, it ceases to be any more the Object either of Jealousy or Resentment of the rest; but if any of the united Powers erect themselves upon the Ruin of that; or by any other method set themselves up too high; the Nuisance is transposed to that Power, which before it was thought convenient to assist, and it becomes as necessary to the rest to reduce that Power or Prince, as it was before to reduce the other.

Thus the *Spanish* Power, in Queen *Elizabeth's* Time grew formidable to *Europe*, and all the Princes, who took Umbrage at their Greatness, confederated with *France* and *England* to reduce it.

The *Austrian* Power in the Emperor *Ferdinand* II became formidable to *Europe*; whereupon all the Protestant Princes agreed to call in, and assist the King of *Sweden*, in bringing the *Germans* to due Bounds, and to harken to Reason, and *England, France*, and *Holland* jointly concurred.

France from these Fractions and Quarrels among the Protestants, established its Greatness, and raised herself on the Ruin of its so potent Neighbours, till the most exquisite Conduct of the present King has brought that Greatness to a too formidable Height; and thereby placed her in the envied Seat of Power, which standing without the Circle of Mediocrity makes her uneasy to all the rest.

Should any of the Branches of the present Confederacy push at a Conquest, and by the Advantage of the falling Greatness of the *French* power, engross to themselves a Dominion too large, or any Superiority of Power above his proper Sphere, that very Power or Prince would in his Degree become equally obnoxious to the rest, and the Balance of Power being thereby broken, would be as much the public Enemy as the *French* are now . . .

---

[1] *Review*, 28th May 1706.
[2] *Review*, 30th May 1706. Both issues extol the victories of the Duke of Marlborough against the French.

THE DUKE OF BERRY

RENUNCIATION OF THE SPANISH CROWN (1712)

[From: Henri Vast, *Les Grands traités du regne de Louis XIV*, iii. Paris 1899. p. 54. Translated by the editor.]

This statement, signed in Paris on 24th November 1712, was one of three 'renunciations' by means of which the separation of the crowns of France and Spain was assured at the close of the War of the Spanish Succession. The other two renunciations were made by Philip of Anjou, who in accepting the Spanish crown gave up his rights of succession to his grandfather, Louis XIV; and by Louis XIV's brother, Philip Duke of Orléans, who renounced any pretensions to the Spanish crown. The language is similar to the Anglo-Spanish treaty of 2nd–13th July 1713, whose objective was to establish an 'exact balance of power, which is the best and firmest basis of mutual friendship and enduring concord in every respect'.

It has been agreed among the Most Christian King, our most-honoured lord and grandfather; [1] King Philip V, our brother; [2] and the Queen of Great Britain [3] that the said King Philip will renounce for himself and for all his descendants the hope of succeeding to the crown of France; that for our part we will also renounce for us and our descendants the crown of Spain; that the Duke of Orléans, our very dear uncle, will do the same thing, so that all the lines of France and Spain respectively, and relatively, will be excluded for always and in any manner from all the rights which the lines of France might have to the crown of Spain, and the lines of Spain to the crown of France; and finally that the house of Austria will be prevented, whether under the pretext of these renunciations or any other pretext, from exercising the pretensions which she might have to the succession of the monarchy of Spain; all the more that in uniting this monarchy to the countries and hereditary states of this house [Austria], it would be formidable, even without the union of the Empire, [4] to the other Powers who are in the middle and would find themselves as it were surrounded. This would destroy the equality which is being established today to assure and affirm more perfectly the peace of Christianity, and to remove all jealousies from the Powers of the North and West, which is the goal proposed by this political equilibrium, in separating and excluding thus all these branches, and calling to the crown of Spain, in default of the lines of King Philip V, our brother, and of all his children and descendants, the house of the Duke of Savoy who descends from the Infanta Catherine, daughter of Philip II. It has been considered that in causing thus to succeed immediately the said house of Savoy, we can establish as it were in its centre this equality and this equilibrium among these three Powers without which we could not extinguish the fire of war which is alight and capable of ruining everyone.

[1] Louis XIV.
[2] King of Spain.
[3] Queen Anne.
[4] Holy Roman Empire.

VISCOUNT BOLINGBROKE

[From: *Letters on the Study and Use of History*. London 1889. (The Victoria Library 3.) pp. 171–81. The letters were written in 1735–6, printed privately in 1738 and eventually published in 1752.]

Henry St John (1678–1751), later Viscount Bolingbroke, was a Tory leader during the reign of Queen Anne and chief architect of the Peace of Utrecht (1713), which he sought to defend in his *Letters on the Study and Use of History*, written in 1735–6. He divided modern history into three periods: '1. From the fifteenth to the end of the sixteenth century. 2. From thence to the Pyrenean treaty [1659]. 3. From thence down to the present time.' At the beginning of his account of the third period in Letter VII he makes some general observations on the balance of power in Europe, 'on the equal poize of which the safety and tranquillity of all must depend' (Letter VI).

The first observation I shall make on this third period of modern history is, that as the ambition of Charles V, who united the whole formidable power of Austria in himself, and the restless temper, the cruelty and bigotry of Philip II, were principally objects of the attention and solicitude of the councils of Europe, in the first of these periods; and as the ambition of Ferdinand II and III, who aimed at nothing less than extirpating the Protestant interest, and under that pretence subduing the liberties of Germany, were objects of the same kind in the second: so an opposition to the growing power of France, or to speak more properly to the exorbitant ambition of the house of Bourbon, has been the principal affair of Europe during the greatest part of the present period. The design of aspiring to universal monarchy was imputed to Charles V, as soon as he began to give proofs of his ambition and capacity. The same design was imputed to Louis XIV, as soon as he began to feel his own strength, and the weakness of his neighbours. Neither of these princes was induced, I believe, by the flattery of his courtiers, or the apprehensions of his adversaries, to entertain so chimerical a design as this would have been, even in that false sense wherein the word universal is so often understood: and I mistake very much if either of them was of a character, or in circumstances, to undertake it. Both of them had strong desires to raise their families higher, and to extend their dominions farther; but neither of them had that bold and adventurous ambition which makes a conqueror and a hero. These apprehensions, however, were given wisely, and taken usefully. They cannot be given nor taken too soon when such powers as these arise; because when such powers as these are besieged as it were early, by the common policy and watchfulness of their neighbours, each of them may in his turn of strength sally forth and gain a little ground; but none of them will be able to push their conquests far, and much less to consummate the entire projects of their ambition. Besides the occasional opposition that was given to Charles V by our Henry VIII, according to the different moods of humour he was in; by the Popes, according to the several turns of their private interest; and by the princes of Germany, according to the occasions or pretences that religion or civil liberty furnished; he had from his first setting out a rival and an enemy in Francis I, who did not maintain his cause 'in forma pauperis', if I may use such an expression: as we have seen the house of

Austria sue, in our days, for dominion at the gate of every palace in Europe. Francis I was the principal in his own quarrels, paid his own armies, fought his own battles; and though his valour alone did not hinder Charles V from subduing all Europe, as Bayle, a better philologer than politician, somewhere asserts, but a multitude of other circumstances easily to be traced in history; yet he contributed by his victories, and even by his defeats, to waste the strength and check the course of that growing power. Louis XIV had no rival of this kind in the house of Austria, nor indeed any enemy of this importance to combat, till the Prince of Orange became King of Great Britain: and he had great advantages in many other respects, which it is necessary to consider in order to make a true judgment on the affairs of Europe from the year 1660. You will discover the first of these advantages, and such as were productive of all the rest, in the conduct of Richelieu and of Mazarin. Richelieu formed the great design, and laid the foundations: Mazarin pursued the design, and raised the superstructure. If I do not deceive myself extremely, there are few passages in history that deserve your lordship's attention more than the conduct that the first and greatest of these ministers held, in laying the foundations I speak of. You will observe how he helped to embroil affairs on every side, and to keep the house of Austria at bay as it were; how he entered into the quarrels of Italy against Spain, into that concerning the Valteline, and that concerning the succession of Mantua; without engaging so deep as to divert him from another great object of his policy, subduing Rochelle and disarming the Huguenots. You will observe how he turned himself, after this was done, to stop the progress of Ferdinand in Germany. While Spain fomented discontents at the court and disorders in the kingdom of France by all possible means, even by taking engagements with the Duke of Rohan, and for supporting the Protestants; Richelieu abetted the same interest in Germany against Ferdinand; and in the Low Countries against Spain. The emperor was become almost the master in Germany. Christian IV, King of Denmark, had been at the head of a league, wherein the United Provinces, Sweden, and Lower Saxony entered, to oppose his progress; but Christian had been

defeated by Tilly and Valstein, and obliged to conclude a
treaty at Lubec, where Ferdinand gave him the law. It was
then that Gustavus Adolphus, with whom Richelieu made an
alliance, entered into this war, and soon turned the fortune
of it. The French minister had not yet engaged his master
openly in the war; but when the Dutch grew impatient, and
threatened to renew their truce with Spain, unless France
declared; when the King of Sweden was killed, and the battle
of Nordlingen lost; when Saxony had turned again to the side
of the emperor, and Brandenburg and so many others had
followed this example, that Hesse almost alone persisted in the
Swedish alliance: then Richelieu engaged his master, and
profited of every circumstance which the conjuncture afforded,
to engage him with advantage. For, first, he had a double
advantage by engaging so late: that of coming fresh into the
quarrel against a wearied and almost exhausted enemy; and
that of yielding to the impatience of his friends, who, pressed
by their necessities and by the want they had of France, gave
this minister an opportunity of laying those claims and establishing those pretensions in all his treaties with Holland,
Sweden, and the princes and states of the empire, on which
he had projected the future aggrandizement of France. The
manner in which he engaged, and the air that he gave to his
engagement, were advantages of the second sort, advantages
of reputation and credit; yet were these of no small moment
in the course of the war, and operated strongly in favour of
France, as he designed they should, even after his death, and
at and after the treaties of Westphalia. He varnished ambition
with the most plausible and popular pretences. The Elector
of Treves had put himself under the protection of France: and,
if I remember right, he made this step when the emperor
could not protect him against the Swedes, whom he had
reason to apprehend. No matter, the Governor of Luxemburg
was ordered to surprise Treves and to seize the elector. He
executed his orders with success, and carried this prince
prisoner into Brabant. Richelieu seized the lucky circumstance;
he reclaimed the elector: and, on the refusal of the cardinal
infant, the war was declared. France, you see, appeared the
common friend of liberty, the defender of it in the Low

Countries against the King of Spain, and in Germany against
the emperor, as well as the protector of the princes of the
empire, many of whose states had been illegally invaded, and
whose persons were no longer safe from violence even in their
own palaces. All these appearances were kept up in the negotiations at Munster, where Mazarin reaped what Richelieu
had sowed. The demands that France made for herself were
very great; but the conjuncture was favourable, and she
improved it to the utmost. No figure could be more flattering
than hers, at the head of these negotiations; nor more mortify-
ing than the emperor's through the whole course of the treaty.
The princes and states of the empire had been treated as
vassals by the emperor; France determined them to treat with
him on this occasion as sovereigns, and supported them in this
determination. Whilst Sweden seemed concerned for the
Protestant interest alone, and showed no other regard, as she
had no other alliance; France affected to be impartial alike
to the Protestant and to the Papist, and to have no interest at
heart but the common interest of the Germanic body. Her
demands were excessive, but they were to be satisfied principally out of the emperor's patrimonial dominions. It had
been the art of her ministers to establish this general maxim
on many particular experiences, that the grandeur of France
was a real, and would be a constant security to the rights and
liberties of the empire against the emperor; and it is no wonder
therefore, this maxim prevailing, injuries, resentments, and
jealousies being fresh on one side, and services, obligations,
and confidence on the other, that the Germans were not unwilling France should extend her empire on this side of the
Rhine, whilst Sweden did the same on this side of the Baltic.
These treaties, and the immense credit and influence that
France had acquired by them in the empire, put it out of the
power of one branch of the house of Austria to return the
obligations of assistance to the other in the war that continued
between France and Spain till the Pyrenean treaty. By this
treaty the superiority of the house of Bourbon over the house
of Austria was not only completed and confirmed, but the
great design of uniting the Spanish and the French monarchies
under the former was laid.

The third period therefore begins by a great change of the balance of power in Europe, and by the prospect of one much greater and more fatal. Before I descend into the particulars I intend to mention of the course of affairs and of the political conduct of the great powers of Europe in this third period, give me leave to cast my eyes once more back on the second. The reflection I am going to make seems to me important, and leads to all that is to follow.

The Dutch made their peace separately at Munster with Spain, who acknowledged then the sovereignty and independency of their commonwealth. The French, who had been, after our Elizabeth, their principal support, reproached them severely for this breach of faith. They excused themselves in the best manner and by the best reasons they could. All this your lordship will find in the monuments of that time. But I think it not improbable that they had a motive you will not find there, and which it was not proper to give as a reason or excuse to the French. Might not the wise men amongst them consider even then, besides the immediate advantages that accrued by this treaty to their commonwealth, that the imperial power was fallen; that the power of Spain was vastly reduced; that the house of Austria was nothing more than the shadow of a great name, and that the house of Bourbon was advancing, by large strides, to a degree of power as exorbitant and as formidable as that of the other family had been in the hands of Charles V, of Philip II, and lately of the two Ferdinands? Might they not foresee, even then, what happened in the course of very few years, when they were obliged, for their own security, to assist their old enemies the Spaniards against their old friends the French? I think they might. Our Charles I was no great politician, and yet he seemed to discern that the balance of power was turning in favour of France, some years before the treaties of Westphalia. He refused to be neuter, and threatened to take part with Spain, if the French pursued the design of besieging Dunkirk and Graveline, according to a concert taken between them and the Dutch, and in pursuance of a treaty for dividing the Spanish Low Countries, which Richelieu had negotiated. Cromwell either did not discern this turn of the balance of power, long afterwards when it was

much more visible; or, discerning it, he was induced by reasons
of private interest to act against the general interest of Europe.
Cromwell joined with France against Spain, and though he
got Jamaica and Dunkirk, he drove the Spaniards into a
necessity of making a peace with France, that has disturbed
the peace of the world almost fourscore years, and the consequences of which have well-nigh beggared in our times the
nation he enslaved in his. There is a tradition, I have heard
it from persons who lived in those days, and I believe it came
from Thurloe, that Cromwell was in treaty with Spain, and
ready to turn his arms against France when he died. If this
fact was certain, as little as I honour his memory, I should
have some regret that he died so soon. But whatever his intentions were, we must charge the Pyrenean treaty, and the fatal
consequences of it, in great measure to his account. The
Spaniards abhorred the thought of marrying their Infanta to
Louis XIV. It was on this point that they broke the negotia-
tion Lionne had begun: and your lordship will perceive, that
if they resumed it afterwards, and offered the marriage they
had before rejected, Cromwell's league with France was a
principal inducement to this alteration of their resolutions.

The precise point at which the scales of power turn, like that
of the solstice in either tropic, is imperceptible to common
observation: and, in one case as in the other, some progress
must be made in the new direction before the change is per-
ceived. They who are in the sinking scale, for in the political
balance of power, unlike to all others, the scale that is empty
sinks, and that which is full rises; they who are in the sinking
scale do not easily come off from the habitual prejudices of
superior wealth, or power, or skill, or courage, nor from the
confidence that these prejudices inspire. They who are in the
rising scale do not immediately feel their strength, nor assume
that confidence in it which successful experience gives them
afterwards. They who are the most concerned to watch the
variations of this balance, misjudge often in the same manner,
and from the same prejudices. They continue to dread a power
no longer able to hurt them, or they continue to have no
apprehensions of a power that grows daily more formidable.
Spain verified the first observation at the end of the second

period, when, proud and poor, and enterprising and feeble, she still thought herself a match for France. France verified the second observation at the beginning of the third period, when the triple alliance stopped the progress of her arms, which alliances much more considerable were not able to effect afterwards. The other principal powers of Europe, in their turns, have verified the third observation in both its parts, through the whole course of this period . . .

The Mid-Eighteenth Century

DAVID HUME
OF THE BALANCE OF POWER (1752)

[From: *Essays, Literary, Moral and Political*, 1870. pp. 198–203.]

David Hume (1711–1776), Scottish philosopher and historian, was personally involved in European politics as secretary to General St Claire from 1746 to 1749 on a military expedition to Brittany and a diplomatic mission to Turin; as private secretary to Lord Hertford, British Ambassador in Paris, 1763–6; and as undersecretary of state in the Northern Department, 1767–8. First published in his *Political Discourses* (1752), Hume's essay on the balance of power is undoubtedly the most famous on this theme. It is chiefly distinguished by its discussion of the idea in classical antiquity.

It is a question whether the *idea* of the balance of power be owing entirely to modern policy, or whether the *phrase* only has been invented in the later ages? It is certain that Xenophon in his Institution of Cyrus, represents the combination of the Asiatic powers to have arisen from a jealousy of the increasing force of the Medes and Persians: and though that elegant composition should be supposed altogether a romance, this sentiment, ascribed by the author to the Eastern princes, is at least a proof of the prevailing notion of ancient times.

In all the politics of Greece, the anxiety, with regard to the balance of power, is apparent, and is expressly pointed out to us, even by the ancient historians. Thucydides represents the league which was formed against Athens, and which produced the Peloponnesian war, as entirely owing to this principle. And after the decline of Athens, when the Thebans and Lace-demonians disputed for sovereignty, we find that the Athenians (as well as many other republics) always threw themselves into the lighter scale, and endeavoured to preserve the balance. They supported Thebes against Sparta, till the great victory gained by Epaminondas at Leuctra; after which they immediately went over to the conquered, from generosity, as they pretended, but in reality from their jealousy of the conquerors.

Whoever will read Demosthenes's oration for the Megalopolitans, may see the utmost refinements on this principle, that ever entered into the head of a Venetian or English speculatist. And upon the first rise of the Macedonian power, this orator immediately discovered the danger, sounded the alarm throughout all Greece, and at last assembled that confederacy under the banners of Athens, which fought the great and decisive battle of Chaeronea.

It is true, the Grecian wars are regarded by historians as wars of emulation rather than of politics; and each state seems to have had more in view the honour of leading the rest, than any well-grounded hopes of authority and dominion. If we consider, indeed, the small number of inhabitants in any one republic, compared to the whole, the great difficulty of forming sieges in those times, and the extraordinary bravery and discipline of every freeman among that noble people; we shall conclude, that the balance of power was, of itself, sufficiently secured in Greece, and need not to have been guarded with that caution which may be requisite in other ages. But whether we ascribe the shifting of sides in all the Grecian republics to *jealous emulation* or *cautious politics*, the effects were alike, and every prevailing power was sure to meet with a confederacy against it, and that often composed of its former friends and allies.

The same principle, call it envy or prudence, which produced the *Ostracism* of Athens, and *Petalism* of Syracuse, and expelled every citizen whose fame or power overtopped the rest; the same principle, I say, naturally discovered itself to foreign politics, and soon raised enemies to the leading state, however moderate in the exercise of its authority.

The Persian monarch was really, in his force, a petty prince compared to the Grecian republics; and therefore it behoved him, from views of safety more than from emulation, to interest himself in their quarrels, and to support the weaker side in every contest. This was the advice given by Alcibiades to Tissaphernes and it prolonged, near a century, the date of the

Persian empire; till the neglect of it for a moment, after the
first appearance of the aspiring genius of Philip, brought that
lofty and frail edifice to the ground, with a rapidity of which
there are few instances in the history of mankind.

The successors of Alexander showed great jealousy of the
balance of power; a jealousy founded on true politics and
prudence, and which preserved distinct for several ages the
partition made after the death of that famous conqueror. The
fortune and ambition of Antigonus threatened them anew
with a universal monarchy; but their combination, and their
victory at Ipsus, saved them. And in subsequent times, we
find, that, as the Eastern princes considered the Greeks and
Macedonians as the only real military force with whom they
had any intercourse, they kept always a watchful eye over
that part of the world. The Ptolemies, in particular, supported
first Aratus and the Achæans, and then Cleomenes king of
Sparta, from no other view than as a counterbalance to the
Macedonian monarchs. For this is the account which Polybius
gives of the Egyptian politics.

The reason why it is supposed that the ancients were entirely
ignorant of the *balance of power*, seems to be drawn from the
Roman history more than the Grecian; and as the transactions
of the former are generally more familiar to us, we have thence
formed all our conclusions. It must be owned, that the Romans
never met with any such general combination or confederacy
against them, as might naturally have been expected for their
rapid conquests and declared ambition, but were allowed
peaceably to subdue their neighbours, one after another, till
they extended their dominion over the whole known world.
Not to mention the fabulous history of their Italic wars, there
was, upon Hannibal's invasion of the Roman state, a remark-
able crisis, which ought to have called up the attention of all
civilized nations. It appeared afterwards (nor was it difficult
to be observed at the time) that this was a contest for universal
empire; yet no prince or state seems to have been in the least
alarmed about the event or issue of the quarrel. Philip of
Macedon remained neuter, till he saw the victories of Hannibal; and then most imprudently formed an alliance with the
conqueror, upon terms still more imprudent. He stipulated,

that he was to assist the Carthaginian state in their conquest of Italy; after which they engaged to send over forces into Greece, to assist him in subduing the Grecian commonwealth.

The Rhodian and Achæan republics are much celebrated by ancient historians for their wisdom and sound policy; yet both of them assisted the Romans in their wars against Philip and Antiochus. And what may be esteemed still a stronger proof, that this maxim was not generally known in those ages, no ancient author has remarked the imprudence of these measures, nor has even blamed that absurd treaty abovementioned, made by Philip with the Carthaginians. Princes and statesmen, in all ages, may, beforehand, be blinded in their reasonings with regard to events: but it is somewhat extraordinary, that historians, afterwards, should not form a sounder judgment of them.

Massinissa, Attalus, Prusias, in gratifying their private passions, were all of them the instruments of the Roman greatness, and never seem to have suspected, that they were forging their own chains, while they advanced the conquests of their ally. A simple treaty and agreement between Massinissa and the Carthaginians, so much required by mutual interest, barred the Romans from all entrance into Africa, and preserved liberty to mankind.

The only prince we meet with in the Roman history, who seems to have understood the balance of power, is Hiero, king of Syracuse. Though the ally of Rome, he sent assistance to the Carthaginians during the war of the auxiliaries; 'Esteeming it requisite,' says Polybius, both in order to retain his dominions in Sicily, 'and to preserve the Roman friendship, that Carthage should be safe; lest by its fall the remaining power should be able, without contrast or opposition, to execute every purpose and undertaking. And here he acted with great wisdom and prudence: for that is never, on any account, to be overlooked; nor ought such a force ever to be thrown into one hand, as to incapacitate the neighbouring states from defending their rights against it.' Here is the aim of modern politics pointed out in express terms.

In short, the maxim of preserving the balance of power is

founded so much on common sense and obvious reasoning, that it is impossible it could altogether have escaped antiquity, where we find, in other particulars, so many marks of deep penetration and discernment. If it was not so generally known and acknowledged as at present, it had at least an influence on all the wiser and more experienced princes and politicians. And indeed, even at present, however generally known and acknowledged among speculative reasoners, it has not, in practice, an authority much more extensive among those who govern the world.

After the fall of the Roman empire, the form of government, established by the northern conquerors, incapacitated them, in a great measure, for farther conquests, and long maintained each state in its proper boundaries. But when vassalage and the feudal militia were abolished, mankind were anew alarmed by the danger of universal monarchy, from the union of so many kingdoms and principalities in the person of the Emperor Charles. But the power of the house of Austria, founded on extensive but divided dominions; and their riches, derived chiefly from mines of gold and silver, were more likely to decay, of themselves, from internal defects, than to overthrow all the bulwarks raised against them. In less than a century, the force of that violent and haughty race was shattered, their opulence dissipated, their splendor eclipsed. A new power succeeded, more formidable to the liberties of Europe, possessing all the advantages of the former, and labouring under none of its defects, except a share of that spirit of bigotry and persecution, with which the house of Austria was so long, and still is so much infatuated.

In the general wars maintained against this ambitious power, Great Britain has stood foremost, and she still maintains her station. Beside her advantages of riches and situation, her people are animated with such a national spirit, and are so fully sensible of the blessings of their government, that we may hope their vigour never will languish in so necessary and so just a cause. On the contrary, if we may judge by the past, their passionate ardour seems rather to require some moderation; and they have more often erred from a laudable excess than from a blameable deficiency.

1. We seem to have been more possessed with the ancient Greek spirit of jealous emulation, than actuated by the prudent views of modern politics. Our wars with France have been begun with justice, and even perhaps from necessity, but have always been too far pushed, from obstinacy and passion. The same peace, which was afterwards made at Ryswick in 1697, was offered so early as the year 1692; that concluded at Utrecht in 1712 might have been finished on as good conditions at Gertruytenberg in 1708; and we might have given at Frankfort, in 1743, the same terms which we were glad to accept of at Aix-la-Chapelle in the year 1748. Here then we see, that above half of our wars with France, and all our public debts, are owing more to our own imprudent vehemence, than to the ambition of our neighbours.

2. We are so declared in our opposition to French power, and so alert in defence of our allies, that they always reckon upon our force as upon their own; and expecting to carry on war at our expense, refuse all reasonable terms of accommodation. *Habent subjectos, tamquam suos; viles, ut alienos.*[1] All the world knows, that the factious vote of the House of Commons, in the beginning of the last parliament, with the professed humour of the nation, made the Queen of Hungary inflexible in her terms, and prevented that agreement with Prussia, which would immediately have restored the general tranquillity of Europe.

3. We are such true combatants, that, when once engaged, we lose all concern for ourselves and our posterity, and consider only how we may best annoy the enemy. To mortgage our revenues at so deep a rate in wars where we were only accessories, was surely the most fatal delusion, that a nation, which had any pretensions to politics and prudence, has ever yet been guilty of. That remedy of funding, if it be a remedy, and not rather a poison, ought, in all reason, to be reserved to the last extremity; and no evil, but the greatest and most urgent, should ever induce us to embrace so dangerous an expedient.

These excesses, to which we have been carried, are prejudicial, and may, perhaps, in time, become still more prejudicial another way, by begetting, as is usual, the opposite extreme, and rendering us totally careless and supine with regard to the fate of Europe. The Athenians, from the most bustling, intriguing, warlike, people of Greece, finding their error in thrusting themselves into every quarrel, abandoned all attention to foreign affairs; and in no contest ever took part on either side, except by their flatteries and complaisance to the victor.

Enormous monarchies are, probably, destructive to human nature; in their progress, in their continuance, and even in their downfall, which never can be very distant from their establishment. The military genius, which aggrandized the monarchy, soon leaves the court, the capital, and the centre of such a government: while the wars are carried on at a great distance, and interest so small a part of the state. The ancient nobility, whose affections attach them to their sovereign, live all at court; and never will accept of military employments which would carry them to remote and barbarous frontiers, where they are distant both from their pleasures and their fortune. The arms of the state must therefore be entrusted to mercenary strangers, without zeal, without attachment, without honour; ready on every occasion to turn them against the prince, and join each desperate malcontent who offers pay and plunder. This is the necessary progress of human affairs: thus human nature checks itself in its airy elevation; thus ambition blindly labours for the destruction of the conqueror, of his family, and of every thing near and dear to him. The Bourbons, trusting to the support of their brave, faithful, and affectionate nobility, would push their advantage without reserve or limitation. These, while fired with glory and emulation, can bear the fatigues and dangers of war; but never would submit to languish in the garrison of Hungary or Lithuania, forgot at court, and sacrificed to the intrigues of every minion or mistress who approaches the prince. The troops are filled with Cravates and Tartars, Hussars and Cossacks, intermingled, perhaps, with a few soldiers of fortune from the better provinces: and the melancholy fate of the Roman emperors, from the same cause, is renewed over and over again, till the final dissolution of the monarchy.

[1] 'They treat (us) as if they were our masters, and despise (us) as outsiders' (Tacitus, *Histories* i.37).

ANTOINE PECQUET

OPINIONS ON THE BALANCE OF POWER

[From: *L'Esprit des Maximes politiques pour servir de suite à L'Esprit des loix, du Président de Montesquieu.* Paris 1757. Book 1, Chapter 12, pp. 191–206, with minor omissions. Translated by John Warrington.]

Antoine Pecquet (1704–1762) was a man of letters who served for a time in the French Office of Foreign Affairs and wrote a manual on the art of negotiating with sovereigns. His *L'Esprit des Maximes politiques* (1757) was somewhat pretentiously written as a sequel to Montesquieu's *L'Esprit des lois.* The chapter on the balance of power alludes to the criticisms which had already been made of the idea, and outlines the main considerations to be taken into account.

This important subject, in the process of being well nigh exhausted, has become perhaps even more obscure because it has been approached from somewhat ill-defined viewpoints. Even today, in fact, many discuss the 'equilibrium of Europe' but seldom understand much about it, or look for it where it might be supposed to lie. Meanwhile the words are on everybody's lips: a weak or timid government, one state jealous of another, sounds the tocsin with this single phrase. At such moments of alarm we hear on all sides that the balance has been lost, that Europe and its system have been overturned. Everyone panics at this general cry. Some suggest that the balance can be restored in one way, some in another. Ask each in turn where this much-invoked deity resides, what is necessary to constitute this equilibrium, how it can be preserved, and what reliable system can establish it when it has unfortunately suffered some disturbance. I doubt whether anyone will be able to give you an answer.

Personally, I think it is easier to define wherein it does *not* consist than where it does. Since it is highly subjective, residing largely in the opinion of men and in the operation of secondary causes upon which it is physically impossible to establish fixed and variable principles, *I believe it to exist whenever I see states living together at peace and not threatening one another with destruction.* In such cases I feel no trepidation; I believe

I am doing everything required for the balance of power whenever I strive to preserve this universal peace, or, if I cannot prevent it from being disturbed, to re-establish it more firmly.

It seems to me necessary, therefore, to discuss this matter of equilibrium (whatever it may be) at some length, because it is necessarily involved in all the relationships upon which we have proposed to base the spirit of political maxims, and because it is in fact the most essential and most important objective of politics ; because it is, so to speak, their masterpiece, and because every statesman who has not himself assailed or allowed others to assail the balance of power in Europe will deserve the reputation of a great man.

This balance is not created by physical equality between the Powers, like two equal weights on a pair of scales. This supposed equality of strength, even if it could be physically established, would indeed be of no more than theoretical value in any attempt to bring about equilibrium. All size, force and power are relative ; forces essentially are nothing but what they are made to achieve, and their balance can be estimated exactly only by the more or less judicious and intelligent use one makes of them. Consequently one may say that the equilibrium depends almost as much upon secondary as upon primary causes. Thus it can and must often vary ; it would often be necessary to remove something from or replace something onto one side of the scales, and that is impossible. The only way to compensate for this impossibility is the combination of several against one, and therein consists the political machinery which, for good or ill, occupies so many minds . . .

It seems to me that this balance could never be entirely broken or upset unless there existed in the political order a Power in the situation of needing no one else, while everyone else had need of her. In that situation the influence of secondary causes might be much more dangerous, because such a Power could easily tyrannize over all others, and because it might perhaps be not unreasonable to fear her on the grounds that men generally do whatever evil they can, and that it is safer not to allow them the means than to take the chance of their being virtuous. But this kind of Power, which we have just supposed, can hardly exist; and it is no doubt due to the wisdom of Providence that there is no Power that can entirely dispense with others.

The preponderance or superiority of some over the rest can therefore be measured according to the proportion of these reciprocal needs. One state, having exposed and ill-secured frontiers, needs the friendship of her neighbours. Another, with inconsiderable revenues, has recourse to the subsidies which he stipulates. One has a weak army, and so comes to terms with those who can furnish him with troops. Another, requiring foreign foodstuffs and merchandise, lives at peace with countries whose soil or industry can supply her with them. Yet another has great abundance of foodstuffs and merchandise which she must sell abroad, and therefore keeps doors open for exploitation through the ordinary channels of trade.

Thus the impossibility of self-sufficiency forms the bond of mutual peace, and both the principle and the support of the equilibrium; indeed it is its surest imaginable support because it is a permanent, necessary, essential interest, to which every fantasy and every passion must yield.

The European balance of power must also be assessed by the use of forces, and this belongs to the class of secondary causes of which we have been speaking. Twenty thousand well-trained men will be relatively superior to fifty thousand badly disciplined or unwarlike troops. The proximity of one or more weak states is a real advantage. An ambitious and enterprising Power, able to set in motion fifty thousand men, will be temporarily a greater threat to the equilibrium of Europe than will a much greater one guided only by the spirit of peace.

Thus, apart from relative needs, of which we have just spoken, the equilibrium will depend largely upon those who rule, that is, upon their passions or their talents; for, passions being equal, a difference of talents will produce a great difference in the diplomatic game. A Power better governed than others, shifting the real balance and that of opinion in its favour, inevitably causes the detailed equilibrium to vary, and, in a greater or lesser degree, calls the attention of those

others to public events. Of the possible variations in the
equilibrium it is this one against which it is more difficult to
decide what precautions to take. It is legitimate in the public
sphere to derive the greatest possible advantage from one's
situation provided that by so doing one harms no one else.
Would one then be entitled to invoke the interests of the
equilibrium? Only within itself can a state find the means of
re-establishing and preserving proportion in its relationships,
without needing to sound the alarm. . . .

The internal constitution is a third important factor in
considering the equilibrium. Granted equal forces, a popular
or republican government, in which resolutions and executive
orders will depend on the agreement of several minds, will
weigh less in the scales than a government where everything
proceeds from a single centre and a single will, because in the
latter resolutions will be made more promptly, more secretly,
and will be carried out more rapidly, being less subject to
deliberation and scrutiny. In order to prosper, business should
be conducted neither too quickly nor too slowly. A numerous
body is seldom capable of such method and orderliness, which
are possible only in a government where the right of control
resides in an individual. We must not therefore expect to be
able to find exact rules and geometrical principles in a domain
where everything is (so to speak) opinion, itself subject to
variation, and dependent in its application upon the degree
of good sense possessed by politicians who estimate it more or
less soundly, whenever there are no determinate events to
guide them in their judgment, as for example those which
bring an exorbitant Power under a single head, for then the
argument and the groupings are fully decided, and the reckon-
ing is easy to settle. When Rome had begun to grow, if political
genius had presided in the councils of other peoples, they
would have combined to uphold the system of universal
equilibrium, and would have been able to succeed by acting
in accordance with such evident principles. They awoke too
late, and after they had allowed themselves to be subjugated
one by one, Rome was too powerful to be halted in her career
of conquest.

Disturbance of the equilibrium can sometimes also be the

effect of a disastrous war, leading to the spoliation or undue weakening of a particular Power. Thus on such occasions intelligent statesmen are seen to use all their efforts and resources to prevent the abuse of too great success; and whenever this sensible course has not been followed the result has been some disadvantages which have recoiled on those very people who neglected this essential concern for the equilibrium. After the onerous treaty that secured his freedom, Francis I should have found, as in fact he did, more friends than before the battle of Pavia. The excessive ambition of Charles V was all too clearly revealed by the Treaty of Madrid, and intelligent statesmen could not fail to see this.[1]

Marriage alliances too can occasion those combinations of States which should occupy a considerable place in political observations. There have been certain Powers which could never have made those increases contrary to the general idea of equilibrium, if statesmen had looked to the future and forese n the difference that they would one day make in the European balance.

It is to prevent such misfortunes that statesmen, in default of being able to do better, have devised the expedient of renunciations; the real value of these in relation to the principles of natural law we shall not undertake to discuss here. One must believe them legitimate; at least they are useful, since they can help to maintain the so-called equilibrium of Europe, and are perhaps the only possible means of preventing those increases of strength which could overthrow its foundations. Too much has been written inconclusively on this subject, both for and against, because all these writings have been dictated by private and conflicting interests. . . .

True, the arbitrary system of renunciations has been denounced in the name of hallowed rights and of the principles of natural law, and this seems to admit of no reply. But can the interests of the balance justify no exception? Ought not one to entertain great respect for the general agreement of all nations, which, together, are quite competent to renounce some portion of the Law of Nations which is, so to speak, their Law, their Code and their good, as well as their own work? Each by itself has an equal interest in maintaining what can help to ensure the tranquillity of all; and will it not be true to say that there are cases of unanimity of wishes in which it is more useful to be simply statesman than jurist? The latter finds nothing but difficulties, and sows nothing but thorns. The former devises expedients which, as soon as society at large feels content, should become for all nations a respectable Code sheltered from any threat of harm. To be satisfied with what can ensure concord between all nations is surely to fulfil the designs of Providence, which certainly did not form them for the purpose of mutual destruction.

[1] Emperor Charles V captured King Francis I of France at the battle of Pavia in 1525. Francis agreed to large concessions in the Treaty of Madrid of 1526 in exchange for his release, but reneged on his promises on his return to France.

EMMERICH DE VATTEL

[From: *The Law of Nations or The Principles of Natural Law Applied to the Conduct and to the Affairs of Nations and of Sovereigns.* Translation of the 1758 edition, by Charles G. Fenwick. Washington D.C., Carnegie Institution of Washington, 1916. pp. 251-2.]

Emmerich de Vattel (1714-1767) was a Swiss jurist, publicist and diplomat; he was the principal advisor of King Augustus III of Poland. His fame derives from his influential treatise, *Le droit des gens ou principes de la loi naturelle appliqués . . . aux affaires des nations et les souverains*, first published in 1758 and immediately translated into English. In the extract reprinted here Vattel addresses himself to a problem similar to the one discussed by Gentili in an earlier passage: 'Whether the aggrandizement of a neighbouring power can authorize a state to make war upon it.' What chiefly distinguishes Vattel's approach from that of his predecessor is his exposition of the idea of a European political system as the framework within which the 'well-known principle of the balance of power' operates.

. . . Europe forms a political system in which the Nations inhabiting this part of the world are bound together by their relations and various interests into a single body. It is no longer, as in former times, a confused heap of detached parts, each of which had but little concern for the lot of the others, and rarely troubled itself over what did not immediately affect it. The constant attention of sovereigns to all that goes on, the custom of resident ministers, the continual negotiations that take place, make of modern Europe a sort of Republic, whose members—each independent, but all bound by a common interest—unite for the maintenance of order and the preservation of liberty. This is what has given rise to the well-known principle of the balance of power, by which is meant an arrangement of affairs so that no State shall be in a position to have absolute mastery and dominate over the others.

The surest means of preserving this balance of power would be to bring it about that no State should be much superior to the others, that all the States, or at least the larger part, should be about equal in strength. This idea has been attributed to Henry IV, but it is one that could not be realized without injustice and violence. And moreover, once this equality were established, how could it be regularly maintained by lawful means? Commerce, industry, the military virtues, would soon put an end to it. The right of inheritance, even in favour of women and their descendants, which has been so absurdly established for succession to the throne, but which after all has been established, would overturn your arrangement.

It is simpler, easier, and more just to have recourse to the method just referred to, of forming alliances in order to make a stand against a very powerful sovereign and prevent him from dominating. This is the plan followed by the sovereigns of Europe at the present day. They look upon the two principal powers, who for that very reason are naturally rivals, as destined to act as a mutual check upon each other, and they unite with the weaker of the two, thereby acting as so much weight thrown into the lighter scale in order to make the balance even. The House of Austria has for a long time been the predominant power; now it is the turn of France. England, whose wealth and powerful navy have given her a very great influence, without, however, causing any State to fear for its liberty, since that power appears to be cured of the spirit of conquest—England, I say, has the honour to hold in her hands the political scales. She is careful to maintain them in equilibrium. It is a policy of great wisdom and justice, and one which will be always commendable, so long as she only makes use of alliances, confederations, and other equally lawful means.

Confederations would be a sure means of preserving the balance of power and thus maintaining the liberty of Nations, if all sovereigns were constantly aware of their true interests, and if they regulated their policy according to the welfare of the State. But powerful sovereigns succeed only too often in winning for themselves partisans and allies who are blindly devoted to their designs. Dazzled by the glitter of a present advantage, seduced by their greed, deceived by unfaithful ministers, how many princes become the instruments of a power which will one day swallow up either themselves or their successors. The safest plan, therefore, is either to weaken one who upsets the balance of power, as soon as a favourable opportunity can be found when we can do so with justice, or, by the use of all upright means, to prevent him from attaining so formidable a degree of power. To this end all Nations should be on their guard above all not to allow him to increase his power by force of arms, and this they are always justified in doing. For if that prince wages an unjust war every Nation has the right to assist the oppressed State; and if he wages a just war, neutral Nations may interpose to bring about a settlement; they may persuade the weak State to offer just satisfaction upon reasonable terms, and may thus prevent it from being subjugated. When one who wages a just war is offered equitable terms, he has all that he can demand. As we shall see later, the justice of his cause never gives him the right to subjugate his enemy, except when this extreme measure becomes necessary to his safety, or when he has no other means of redressing an injury which he has received. Now, that is not the case here, for the Nations that intervene enable him both to insure his safety and to obtain just redress in another manner.

Finally, there is no question but that if that formidable prince is clearly entertaining designs of oppression and conquest, if he betrays his plans by preparations or other advances, other Nations have the right to check him; and if the fortune of war be favourable to them, they may profit by the favourable opportunity to weaken and reduce his strength, which upsets the balance of power and constitutes a menace to the common liberty of all.

This right on the part of Nations is still more evident as against a sovereign who is always ready to take to arms without cause and without plausible pretext, and who is thus a constant disturber of the public peace. . . .

JEAN-JACQUES ROUSSEAU

ABSTRACT OF THE ABBÉ DE SAINT-PIERRE'S PROJECT FOR PERPETUAL PEACE (1761)
Extract

[From: *The Works of J.-J. Rousseau*, x. Translated from the French. Edinburgh 1774. pp. 182–91.]

Jean-Jacques Rousseau (1712–1778) was a French-Swiss philosopher and moralist whose writings managed to offend most of his contemporaries, and led to a series of exiles and increasing madness late in his life. His disenchantment with the predominantly rationalist approach of his era can be seen in his analysis of the European state-system with which he prefaced his account of the Abbé de Saint-Pierre's project for perpetual peace. Unlike natural law theorists such as Fénelon, Rousseau did not consider the balance of power as a principle of an already existing general association of European states, but rather as a necessary precondition for the construction of such an association.

. . . The ancient simulacrum of the Roman Empire has continued to form a kind of union between the members of which it was composed, and Rome possessed another sort of dominion [1] after the dissolution of the Empire. There resulted from this twofold connection a closer society among the nations of Europe, where the centre of the two powers had existed, than in other parts of the world, where the inhabitants are too much dispersed to hold correspondence with each other, and have besides no particular point of union.

Add to this, the peculiar situation of Europe, more equally populous and fertile, better connected in its several parts; the continual admixture of interest, which consanguinity, commerce, arts, and navigation, continually effect between sovereigns; the multitude of rivers, and diversity of their course, which facilitate the communication of different parts; the inconstancy of the inhabitants, which induces them to travel and pass frequently from one country to another; the invention of printing, and prevailing taste for letters, which has formed a community of knowledge and studies; and lastly, the multiplicity and small extent of many states, which added to the calls of luxury, and to the diversity of climates, render the one always necessary to the other; all these things united form in Europe, not merely, as in Asia or Africa, an ideal collection of people, who have nothing in common but a name, but a real society, which has its religion, morals, customs, and even its laws, from which none of the people composing it can separate without causing an immediate disturbance.

To behold, on the other hand, the perpetual dissensions, depredations, usurpations, rebellions, wars, and murders, which are constantly ravaging this respectable abode of philosophers, this brilliant asylum of the arts and sciences; to reflect on the sublimity of our conversation and the meanness of our proceedings, on the humanity of our maxims and the cruelty of our actions, on the meekness of our religion and the horror of our persecutions, on a policy so wise in theory and so absurd in practice, on the beneficence of sovereigns and the misery of their people, on governments so mild and wars so destructive; we are at a loss to reconcile these strange contrarieties, while this pretended fraternity of European nations appears to be only a term of ridicule, serving ironically to express their reciprocal animosity.

And yet, in all this, things only take their natural course; every society destitute of laws or magistrates, every union formed or supported by chance, must necessarily degenerate into quarrels and dissensions upon the first change of circumstances. The ancient union of the European nations has rendered their interests and privileges extremely complicated; they bear against each other in so many points, that the least agitation of any one puts the whole in motion. Their dissensions are also by so much the more fatal as their connections are intimate; while their frequent quarrels are almost as unnatural and cruel as civil wars.

It must be admitted, therefore, that the present relative state of the European powers is a state of war; and that the partial treaties subsisting between some of them, are rather temporary truces, than a state of actual peace: whether it be owing to those treaties having no other guarantees than the contracting parties; or that their respective rights are never duly ascertained, and the pretensions thence subsisting among powers who acknowledge no superior infallibly prove the source of new wars, as soon as different circumstances empower the pretenders to assert their claims.

To this may be added, that the law of nations not being universally concerted and established, having no general principles, and incessantly varying according to time and place, it is full of contradictory maxims, which can never be reconciled but by the right of the strongest: so that the judgment being without a sure guide, and always biased in doubtful cases by self-interest, war becomes sometimes inevitable, even when both parties may be desirous of acting justly. All that can be done, with the best intentions, therefore, is to decide such disputes by force of arms, or to palliate them by temporary treaties. But no sooner is occasion taken to revive the cause or quarrel, than it takes a new form, and all is complication and confusion: the real grounds of the affair are not to be seen; usurpation passes for right, and weakness for injustice; while, amidst the general disorder, every one finds himself insensibly so far displaced, that, if it were possible to recur to the real and primitive right, there would be few sovereigns in Europe who ought not to refund every thing they possess.

Another source of war, less obvious though not less real, is, that things do not change their form in changing their nature; that states which are hereditary in fact, remain elective in appearance; that there are parliaments or national Estates in monarchies, and hereditary leaders in republics; that one power really dependent on another, still preserves the appearance of liberty; that all the subjects of the same sovereign are not governed by the same laws; that the order of succession is different in different provinces of the same state; in fine, that all governments naturally tend to change, without there being a possibility of preventing it. Such are the general and particular causes which connect us for our ruin, and lead us to describe the charms of social virtue with our hands constantly stained with human gore.

The causes of an evil being once known, the remedy, if any such there be, is sufficiently indicated by the same means. It is plain to every one, that society is formed by a coalition of interests; that every dissension arises from an opposition of interests; that, as a thousand fortuitous events may change and modify both the one and the other, it is necessary that every society should possess a coercive force, to direct and concert the movements of its several members, in order to give their common interests and reciprocal engagements the solidity which they could not separately acquire.

It would moreover be a great mistake to hope that such a violent state could ever change, merely from the nature of things and without the assistance of art. The present system of Europe has attained precisely the degree of solidity which may keep it in a perpetual agitation without ever completely subverting it: thus, if our misfortunes cannot be increased, they are still less capable of being put an end to; because no great revolution can now ever happen.

To prove this, as far as it is necessary, we shall begin with taking a general view of the present state of Europe. The situation of the mountains, seas, and rivers, which serve as boundaries to the several nations inhabiting it, seem also to have determined the number and extent of those nations; so that the political order of this part of the world may be said to be, in some respects, the work of nature.

In fact, we are not to suppose that the boasted balance of power in Europe has been actually established; or that anybody has done anything really with a view to support it. It is found, indeed, to exist; and those who find they have not weight enough to destroy it, cover their own particular designs with the pretence of maintaining it. But whether attended to or not, this balance certainly subsists, and needs no other support than itself, without anyone interfering: and even if it were upset for a moment on one side, it would soon be restored on the other: so, that if the princes who are accused of aspiring to universal monarchy, were really so aspiring, they displayed in this particular much more ambition than judgment; for how could they reflect a moment on such a project, without discovering it to be ridiculous? How could they be insensible, that there is no power in Europe so much superior to the rest, as to be able ever to become their master? Those conquerors, who have brought about great revolutions, have always effected it by the sudden march of unexpected armies; by bringing foreign troops, differently trained to war, against people disarmed, divided, or undisciplined: But where shall we find an European prince whose forces the others are not acquainted with? where find one to subdue the rest, when the greatest of them all forms so small a part of the whole, and they are all so vigilant against each other's encroachments? Will any one maintain more troops than all the rest? He can not; or, if he could, he would only be the sooner ruined, or his troops would be so much the worse as they were more numerous. Will he have them better disciplined? They would be less in proportion. Besides military discipline is nearly the same, or shortly will be so, all over Europe. Will he have more money? Pecuniary resources are common, and money never was known to make any great conquests. Will he make a sudden invasion? Want of subsistence, or fortified towns, will every moment oppose his progress. Will he step by step augment his power and dominion? He will then afford his enemies the means of uniting to resist him: time, money, and men will soon fail him. Will he create dissensions among other powers, in order to conquer them one after another? The maxims of European policy render that scheme ineffectual; nor would the least intelligent of princes be taken in such a snare. In short, not one of them having exclusive resources, the resistance he will meet with must at length equal his efforts; and time will soon repair the casualties of fortune, if not with regard to each particular prince, at least with regard to the general system.

Will it be supposed, that two or three potentates might enter into an agreement to subdue the rest? Be it so. These three potentates, whoever they may be, will not possess half the power of all Europe. The other parts will, therefore, certainly unite against them; and to succeed, they must be able to subdue a power greater than themselves. Add to this, that the views of any three such powers are too opposite, and their jealousy of each other too great, ever to permit the forming of such a project; and also, that if they had formed it, and actually begun to put it into execution with success, that very success would sow the seeds of dissension among the allied conquerors, as it would be morally impossible that their conquests should be so equally divided that each should be satisfied with his acquisition : in which case the dissatisfied party would of course oppose the progress of the others; who, for the like reasons also, would soon disagree between themselves.

I much doubt if, since the world existed, there ever were seen three, or even two, great potentates, that cordially united to subdue the rest, without quarrelling about the contingents to be used in the war, or their share of the conquest; and without affording, by their misunderstanding, new resources to the weaker party. Thus, suppose what we will, it is highly improbable that any prince, or league of princes, will hereafter be able to effect any considerable and permanent change in the political state of Europe.

Not that I pretend to say that the Alps and Pyrenees, the Rhine or the Sea, are insurmountable obstacles to ambition : but these obstacles are supported by others, which strengthen them, or serve to bring states back to their former limits, whenever they have been occasionally removed. The present system of Europe has its support, in a great measure, in the play of political negotiations, which almost always balance each other. But it has still more solid support in the Germanic body; situated almost in the centre of Europe, keeping the other parts in awe, and serving more effectually perhaps to the support of its neighbours than to that of its own members;

a body that is formidable to other states on account of its
extent and the number and wealth of its inhabitants, at the
same time that it is useful to all by its constitution; which,
depriving it of the means and inclination of making conquests,
is the rock on which conquerors generally split. It is certain,
that, notwithstanding the defects in the constitution of the
Empire, the balance of power in Europe will never be destroyed so long as that constitution subsists; that no potentate
need be apprehensive of being dethroned by another; but
that the treaty of Westphalia will be always the basis of our
political system. Thus the law of nations, the study of which is
so much cultivated in Germany, appears to be of much greater
importance than is generally imagined; being not only the
law of Germany, but, in some respects, that of all Europe.

But though the present system is unshakeable, it is for that
very reason the more tempestuous; as there subsists between
the European powers a kind of continual action and re-action,
which, without entirely displacing them, keeps them in constant agitation; their efforts being always ineffectual and
always renascent, like the waves of the ocean, which incessantly agitate its surface without changing its level: so that the
people are perpetually harassed without any tangible advantage being derived from it to their sovereign.

It would be easy for me to deduce the same truth from the
particular interests of all the courts in Europe: for I could
readily show, that these interests are so connected as to keep
all their forces mutually respectful. But the notions of wealth
and commerce having given rise to a species of political
fanaticism, they occasion such sudden changes in the apparent
interests of princes, that no stable maxim can be established
upon those which are the true interests; because at present
every thing depends on the economic systems, most of them
whimsical, which pass through the heads of ministers. Be this,
however, as it may, commerce, which tends daily to an equilibrium, depriving some potentates of their exclusive advantages,
deprives them, at the same time, of one of the greatest means
they possessed of giving laws to others. . . .

[1] Rousseau refers here to the temporal authority of the Roman Church.

CHARLES GRAVIER, COMTE DE VERGENNES

MEMOIR OF M. DE VERGENNES AT THE BEGINNING OF THE REIGN OF LOUIS XVI, IN 1774

[From: *Œuvres complètes de M. le Comte de Ségur*, t. 26. *Politique des cabinets de l'Europe*, t. 3. Paris 1825. pp. 146–58. Translated by John Warrington.]

Charles Gravier, Comte de Vergennes (1717–1787) was the principal architect of French foreign policy in the period immediately before the French Revolution. After a number of diplomatic missions (most notably to Turkey from 1755 to 1768), he was appointed minister of foreign affairs by the new French king, Louis XVI, in 1774. This *mémoire* brilliantly surveys the political scene at this point and outlines the principles on which Vergennes was to base his policies. His association of justice with the system of 'general equilibrium' is characteristic of French enlightenment thought (cf. the earlier selection by Fénelon).

The absolute contempt of the principles of justice and decency, which characterizes the conduct and undertakings of certain contemporary powers, should be an urgent matter of serious consideration, and even of precautionary measures on the part of those states which, guided by healthier maxims, do not equate the just with the unjust.

Posterity will find it hard to believe what an outraged Europe now beholds with astonishment: three powers with different and conflicting interests combining, in a monstrous abuse of superior strength, to despoil an innocent State of her richest domains, a State against whom they have no title other than her weakness and her powerlessness to resist the avarice of those who invade her.[1]

If might is right, if convenience is a title, what security will other States henceforth enjoy? If immemorial possession, if solemn treaties which have determined the respective frontiers, can no longer serve to check ambition, how is one to guarantee oneself against surprise and invasion? If political brigandage is to continue, peace will soon be no more than an open door to infidelity and treason. Less than a century ago we saw a European league drench the earth in blood, in order to avenge

the seizure of a few villages. Now Austria, Russia and Prussia
combine to dismember a great kingdom and partition her
provinces; the rest of Europe watches in silent toleration.
England, lately so zealous and so ardent to maintain the
balance of power in equilibrium, appears not even to notice
a combination so calculated to alarm her; the cry of her most
cherished interest cannot even awake her; she sees her trade
with Poland subjected to the King of Prussia's monopoly, and
she dare not protest.

Faced with this wholesale abandonment of true principles,
what attitude could France adopt? To declare herself the
avenger of outrages upon the sacred rights of justice and
property would be the most magnanimous and best suited to
her dignity. But her internal situation should not advise her
and cannot allow her to shoulder so great a responsibility;
the time is past when a firm and vigorous declaration would
have been able to ensure the integrity and possessions of
Poland. A long and possibly disastrous war would be unlikely
at this stage to alter the new state of affairs that has been
permitted to arise.

The King of Prussia [2] had no less reason to anticipate war
than had the court of Vienna; but, more adroit than the
Austrian minister,[3] he took advantage of the latter's pusill-
animity to associate him with the shameful pact to dismember
and in some sort annihilate a State that was useful and never
harmful to the house of Austria, in order to obtain for himself
an increase of power that will henceforth be most disquieting
if not lethal, for the same house.

This opposition of interests between two virtually equal
powers seems to give France less reason for anxiety over the
encroachments they have allowed themselves and which they
may again venture to commit. Since their designs for aggrandizement are limited to the north and east of their respective
states, France has no immediate grounds for anxiety or fear.
She can feel all the more secure in that she will always be able
in the case of need to count upon one of the two in order to
balance them one against the other.

That, no doubt, is the most plausible argument by which a
passive policy can justify its own inaction. But this argument,

which derives its whole strength from the supposedly habitual
division of those Powers, flies in the face of the history of the
most recent events.

During the course of almost two centuries the great Powers
have concentrated all their designs, and devoted almost all
their means towards preventing any of them from becoming
preponderant. A new combination is supplanting that system
of general equilibrium. Three Powers endeavour to establish
a particular one; they found it on the equality of their usurpations. Thus they cause the balance of power to lean strongly in
their favour. There is no reason to think that their avarice is
yet fully satisfied, and consequently that their monstrous
union is ready to dissolve or cannot be given new life. The
King of Prussia is so clever in the art of sowing illusion and
deception that the Emperor [4] is inclined to be taken in whenever his pride can be engaged or his greed flattered. The
Empress-Queen,[5] who thinks with more equity and moderation, will oppose this propensity as much as she dares; but
she may die when least expected. This princess bears within
herself the seed of a dreadful malady; who can be sure, in the
event of her death, that her son the Emperor, whose genius
is no less romantic than his character is ambitious, would not
decide to make good the antiquated pretensions of his crown
and his house to Italy, and perhaps lay claim to the patrimony
of his ancestors? It is futile to flatter oneself that the King of
Prussia would stand in his way; what greater advantage could
he desire than to see the court of Vienna commit its forces
and undermine its strength in an exhausting enterprise, whose
success would appear at the least uncertain? Being a clever
statesman, he would be more likely to foster a situation which
might enable him to achieve conquests less difficult and quite
as useful. Once satisfied this prince would be able to turn again
to France; [6] but that would be later, only when he saw her
ready to yield and he had reason to fear that the power of
Austria, strengthened by large acquisitions, might fall upon
him with the whole weight of its mass.

A no less important consideration which must not be ig-
nored, is that when the Viennese court breaks its links with
France, it will have England as an ally. Both are ready to form

an alliance as soon as some common interest brings them together. England being united with the house of Austria and
sharing its projects and its aims, France will no longer be
able to wage war unless she is ready to do so by sea as well as
by land.

It may be objected, on the one hand, that this forecast is
concerned with matters that are very remote to say the least,
and, on the other, that since the King of Prussia is by his
situation the natural enemy of the house of Austria, it must
be supposed that the latter can light-heartedly decide to
break an alliance of which it is the true beneficiary. This
reflection is perfectly true; but have errors of calculation and
of judgment never before been made? Is not what is now hap-
pening an equally genuine and distressing example? Moreover, if we wish to cling to our allies and be sure of them, their
confidence and their loyalty will always depend upon the
benefit they expect to derive from our alliance, or upon the
fear of our resentment in the event of their failing us, and
consequently upon the more or less favourable idea they have
of our internal situation. Fear and hope have been and always
will be the two mainsprings of the political and the moral
order.

Again, no matter how far distant may be the matters which
we are here concerned to forecast, we must not blind ourselves
to the fact that causes independent of human power can bring
them near. It has already been remarked that the Empress-
Queen may die quite unexpectedly. Are we any more certain
that the opening moves in the succession to Berg and Jülich
and to that of Bavaria will not hasten the ordinary course of
nature? Those are events of whose possibility it is painful to
think, because one cannot shut one's eyes to the fact that they
may lead to war. And there may be many others which foresight cannot yet grasp. The second- and third-rate Powers are
without support, and likely to find themselves engulfed by
those now predominant, when the latter see fit to partition
them. Germany perhaps has no worries, and the North is
tranquil. It may be said that France will be able to abstain
from taking part in the troubles which might arise. But if she
isolates herself; if she renounces her former principles; if,

disregarding her most sacred obligations, the most solemn treaties (notably that of Westphalia) she shows herself indifferent to the fate of her allies and of the princes whose existence she has guaranteed, she must inevitably find herself without allies. Useless to everyone, abandoned by all: that sort of existence cannot guarantee solid and lasting tranquillity.

If, having traversed the continent, we turn our eyes seaward, do we find there greater motives for security? We see alongside us a restless and greedy nation, more jealous of her neighbour's prosperity than of her own happiness, powerfully armed, ready to strike whenever it suits her. Let us not deceive ourselves: whatever parade British ministers may make of their peaceful intentions, we cannot rely on this disposition except while their domestic embarrassments continue. These may pass; they may even increase to a point at which the government decides to direct the prevailing agitation against external objects. It will not be the first time that the cry of war against France has been used to rally the parties which divide England. Further, we may find ourselves involved in a war at sea against the wishes of the court of London as well as of our own. We have a treaty with Spain, who is bound to join us in any war, offensive or defensive. Yet in time of war, Spain's vast overseas possessions often render her more vulnerable than France. The engagement is no doubt extremely burdensome; but, burdensome though it may appear, it may nevertheless be more advantageous to France than to Spain. The useful trade that England does with Spain, which affords an outlet for her own manufactures as well as a source of work and wealth, makes her less keen to seize lands which are cultivated for the benefit of others, whereas having nothing to gain by the exploitation of legitimate trade with France, she beholds with jealous cupidity the wonderful success of our plantations in America and our industry in Europe. If anything holds her back and makes her think twice, it is the thought of France and Spain combined; it is the certainty that the first shot she fires against one or the other will be answered by both.

If, as can hardly be doubted, the remainder of this pact is useful to us, it behoves us to be able to carry out its obligations. Whether it be lack of determination or failure of means that prevents the fulfilment, if the latter is wanting the treaty is *de facto* null and void.

Please God, this may never be the fate of the 'Family Pact'![7] France would be the first to suffer from the deadly recoil; but while she ought to be faithful and true to the terms of this alliance, it is no less important to maintain it fairly so that one of the allies shall not be in the invidious position of demanding everything from the other without feeling bound to take it into consideration. The respect and influence of any Power are measured and regulated according to the opinion entertained of its intrinsic strength. Foresight, then, must endeavour to establish that opinion in the most advantageous sense. Every nation is respected that is seen to be capable of vigorous resistance, but which, not abusing its strength, desires only what is just and can be profitable to everyone—peace and general tranquillity.

Here policy halts. Content to point out the goal to be attained, it does not venture to determine exclusively the choice of ways that lead thereto; but one truth, though trivial, which it cannot neglect to recommend is that, the longer a peace has lasted, the less it seems likely to endure. Peace has existed for twelve years—a strong argument against the probability of its further continuance. To insist, therefore, on the necessity of preparedness for anything that may happen is not to exceed the limits of legitimate foresight. Moreover one is never more certain of peace than when one is in the situation of not fearing war. It is said that opinion is queen of the world. The government which is able to turn it to its own advantage, doubles, along with the idea of its real strength, the consideration and esteem which always will be the reward of a sound administration, and the surest guarantee of its tranquillity.

[1] The first partition of Poland in 1772 by Austria, Prussia and Russia, who invoked the balance of power as justification.

[2] Frederick II.

[3] Kaunitz.

[4] Joseph II.

[5] Maria Theresa, Joseph's mother.

[6] Seeking to revive the pre-1756 alliance between Prussia and France.

[7] The alliance between France and Spain referred to above.

The Napoleonic Wars and their Aftermath

JOHANN GOTTLIEB FICHTE

[From: *The Characteristics of the Present Age*. Translated from the German by William Smith. 2nd edition. London 1859. pp. 208–15. Originally published as *Die Grundzüge des gegenwärtigen Zeitalters*, Berlin 1806.]

Johann Gottlieb Fichte (1762–1814), German philosopher, held professorships at the universities of Jena, Erlangen and Berlin where he developed and expounded his philosophy of ethical idealism. In 1804–5 he delivered a series of popular lectures in Berlin on *The Characteristics of the Present Age*, which included the following account of the balance-of-power system. Fichte's emphasis on universal monarchy is largely inspired by the threat of Napoleonic domination, and his analysis of the elements of power reflects the state-directed socialism he had outlined in *The Closed Commercial State* (1800). He is best known for the theory of nationalism which he advanced in *Addresses to the German Nation* (1808).

... There is a necessary tendency in every cultivated State to extend itself generally, and to include all men within the unity of its Citizenship. Such is the case in Ancient History. In Modern Times a barrier was opposed to this tendency by the internal weakness of the States, and by the Spiritual Central Power [the Papacy], whose interest it was that the Realm of Culture should remain divided. As the States became stronger in themselves and cast off that foreign power, the tendency towards a Universal Monarchy over the whole Christian World necessarily came to light; and this so much the more since it was but one common Culture which had developed in the different States, though with various modifications; and in reference to these particular modifications they had all received but a partial cultivation. In such a state of partial culture, as

87

we have already remarked, each State is tempted to consider
its own civilization as the best, and to imagine that the
inhabitants of other countries would esteem themselves very
fortunate, were they but Citizens of its Realm.

This tendency towards Universal Monarchy, as well as the
conquest of other Christian States, was rendered so much the
easier in this realm of Christendom, inasmuch as the manners
and customs of the European Nations and their Political
Constitutions are almost everywhere alike; besides there are
one or two Languages which are common to the cultivated
classes among all nations, while those which are not so
generally known may, in case of necessity, be easily acquired;
and on this account the conquered, finding themselves in
nearly the same position under their new government as under
the old, take little interest in the question who shall be their
ruler; while the conquerors can thus in a short time, and with
little trouble, recast the new provinces in the form of the old,
and use the former as freely as the latter. Through the Reforma-
tion, indeed, many forms of the one Christianity have arisen;
and among these, in part, a most hostile aversion. But, on the
other hand, each State has the easy remedy of peaceful
Toleration and equal privileges to all; and thus once more, as
formerly in the Heathen Roman Empire, Religious Toleration,
and accommodation in particulars to the manners of other
nations, have become an excellent means of making and
maintaining conquests; while at the same time, the union of
several creeds in one political body efficiently promotes the
purpose which, in our former lecture, we have described as the
absolute purpose of Christianity,—the complete separation of
Religion from the State,—since the State must thus become
neutral and indifferent towards all creeds.

This tendency towards a Christian-European Universal
Monarchy has shown itself successively in the several States
which could make pretensions to such a dominion, and, since
the fall of the Papacy, it has become the sole animating
principle of our History. We by no means seek to determine
whether this notion of Universal Monarchy has ever been
entertained as a definite plan;—the Historian may even bring
forward the negative argument that this thought has never

attained a clear and distinct acceptance in any individual mind, without our principle being thereby overthrown. Whether clearly or not,—it may be obscurely,—yet has this tendency lain at the root of the undertakings of many States in Modern Times, for only by this principle can these undertakings be explained. Many States, already powerful in themselves, and indeed the more on that account, have exhibited an extraordinary desire for yet more extensive dominion, and have sought to acquire new provinces by inter-marriage, treaty, or conquest;—not from the realms of Barbarism, which would give another aspect to the business, but within the empire of Christianity itself. To what purpose did they propose to apply this accession of power, and to what purpose did they actually apply it, when it was attained? To acquire yet more possessions. And where would this progress have had an end, had matters but proceeded according to the desire of these States? Only at the point where there was nothing more left to satiate the desire of acquisition. Although no individual Epoch may have contemplated this purpose, yet is this the spirit which runs through all these individual Epochs, and invisibly urges them onward.

Against this desire of aggrandizement, the less powerful States are now compelled to consider their own preservation; —one condition of which is the preservation of the other States, in order that the power of our natural enemy may not be increased by the acquisition of any of these States to our disadvantage:—in one word, it becomes the business of the less powerful States to maintain a Balance of Power in Christendom. 'What we ourselves cannot acquire, no other shall acquire, because his power would thereby obtain a disproportionate addition'; and thus the care of the great States for their own preservation is at the same time the protection of the weaker communities:—or 'If we cannot hinder others from aggrandizing themselves, then we must also secure for ourselves a proportionate aggrandizement.'

No State, however, strives to maintain this Balance of Power in the European Republic of Nations, except on account of its being unable to attain something more desirable, and because it cannot yet realize the purpose of its own individual aggrand-

izement, and the plan of Universal Monarchy which lies at
the foundation of that purpose;—whenever it becomes more
powerful, it is sure to embrace this design. Thus each State
strives either to attain this Universal Christian Monarchy, or
at least to acquire the power of striving after it;—to maintain
the Balance of Power when it is in danger of being disturbed by
another; and, in secret, for power, that it may eventually
disturb it itself.

This is the natural and necessary course of things, whether
it be confessed or not,—whether it be even recognized or not.
That a State, even when taken on the very point of warfare,
should solemnly assert its love of peace and its aversion to
conquest, alters nothing;—for, in the first place, it must make
this averment, and so hide its real intention, if it would
succeed in its design; and the well-known principle, 'Threaten
war that thou mayest have peace', may also be inverted in this
way—'Promise peace, that thou mayest begin war with
advantage';—and, in the second place, it may be wholly in
earnest with this assurance at the time, so far as it knows itself:
but let the favourable opportunity for aggrandizement present
itself, and the previous good resolution is forgotten. And thus
in the ceaseless struggles of the Christian Republic, do weak
States gradually raise themselves first to an equality, and then
to a superiority, of power; while others which before had
boldly strode onwards to Universal Monarchy, now contend
only for the maintenance of the Balance of Power; and a third
class, who perhaps have formerly occupied both of these
positions, and still remain free and independent with respect
to their internal affairs, have yet, in their external relations
and as regards their political power in Europe, become mere
appendages to other and more powerful States. And so, by
means of these vicissitudes, Nature strives after, and maintains,
an equilibrium, through the very struggles of men for
superiority.

A less powerful State, simply because it is less powerful,
cannot extend itself by foreign conquest. How then shall it
attain any considerable importance within this necessary
limitation? There is no other means possible but the cultivation
of internal strength. Should it not even acquire a single foot of

new ground, yet if its ancient soil be better peopled, richer in all human purposes,—then, without gaining territory, it has gained *men* as the strength and muscle of its State; and should they have come to it from other States, it has won them from its natural rivals. This is the first peaceful conquest, with which each less powerful State in Christian Europe may commence to work out its own elevation;—for the Christian Europeans are essentially but one people, recognize this common Europe as their one true Fatherland, and, from one end of it to the other, pursue nearly the same purposes, and are actuated by similar motives. They seek Personal Freedom, Rights and Laws under which all men shall be equal, and by which all shall be protected without exception or favour; they seek opportunity to earn their subsistence by labour and industry; they seek Religious Toleration for their creeds; Freedom, that they may think according to their own religious and scientific opinions, express these openly, and form their judgments thereby. Where any one of these elements is awanting, thence they long to depart; where these are secured to them, thither they gladly resort. Now all these elements already belong to the necessary purposes of the State as such:—in the present position of individual States towards each other, these purposes are also forced upon it by necessity, and by the care for its own preservation; for the fear of subjugation compels it to self-aggrandizement, and it has, at first, no other means of aggrandizement than that which we have pointed out.

But there is another way by which the State may attract to itself, if not the men of neighbouring States, yet the powers of these men, and may make these powers tributary to itself; and this method plays too important a part in Modern History to be passed over in silence. It consists in a State monopolizing universal Commerce, acquiring exclusive possession of commodities which are generally sought after, and of money, the universal medium of exchange;—thenceforward determining prices for the rest of the world, and so compelling the whole Christian Republic of Nations to pay for those wars which it has from time to time undertaken *against* the whole Christian Republic for the purpose of maintaining this superiority, and to defray the interest of a National Debt contracted for the same purpose. It might possibly be found upon calculation, that when the inhabitant of a country thousands of miles distant has paid for his daily meal, he has spent one-half or three-fourths of the produce of his day's labour for the purposes of this foreign State.—I mention this method, not for the purpose of recommending it; for its success is founded only on the imbecility of the rest of the world, and it would return with fearful retribution upon its inventors were this imbecility removed; but I mention it only in order to point out the remedy against it. This remedy consists in rejecting the use of these commodities; in ceasing to think that the money of this State is the only money; and in believing that a State which has made itself independent in a mercantile respect can make money of what it pleases. But upon this point there is a veil over the eyes of the Age which it is impossible to remove; and it is in vain to waste words on the subject.

When a less powerful State has in the first place acquired internal strength by the methods which we have pointed out, and perhaps thereby become sufficiently powerful to attempt foreign conquest, and, it may be, has succeeded in this undertaking, it then encounters a new difficulty:—it has entirely destroyed the previous Balance of Power and the order of things then existing; and the new comer excites the jealousy and distrust of other States more strongly than those powers with which they are already familiar. It must henceforward be always on its guard, maintain its energies in a state of constant readiness and efficiency, and leave no means unemployed to add at least to its internal strength, when no favourable opportunity presents itself for outward extension. With reference to external affairs, it is a part of this policy to take the weaker neighbouring States under its protection, and thereby make its interest in its own preservation likewise theirs, so that, in succeeding wars, it may be able to calculate upon their power as well as its own. With reference to internal affairs, there are likewise other cares which belong to this policy,—besides the methods which we have already pointed out, of attracting new dwellers to the country, and retaining its old inhabitants;—namely, the care for the preservation and increase of the Human Race, by encouraging marriage and the rearing of children, by sanitary regulations, &c.,—the promotion of the dominion of man over Nature, which we have already sufficiently described, by the systematic and progressive improvement of Agriculture, Industry, and Commerce, and by the maintenance of the necessary equilibrium between these three branches of Business; in short, by all that may be comprehended in the idea of Political Science, when that idea is thoroughly understood. Those who deride such endeavours under the name of *Economy* have only looked upon the outward vesture, and have not penetrated to the essential nature and true meaning of these forms of Business. Among other questions, this one too has been proposed:—Whether the population of a State may not become too large? In our opinion, the indolent and unproductive Citizen is at all times, and in every state of the population, superfluous and unnecessary; but when, with a growing population, Agriculture, Industry, and Commerce also increase in suitable proportions to each other, then the country can never have too many inhabitants; for the productiveness of Nature, when systematically cultivated, is inexhaustible.

All these measures are, as we have shown above, the proper and natural purposes of the State;—in the present State System, however, they are even forced upon it by necessity. It is quite possible that, in what we have now set forth, we may have merely described that which existing States, who lay claim to high culture, actually do and practise; but we have set it forth with a new significance. We have seen that these things are not done by mere chance, but that these States are compelled to do them by necessity; and we have thereby pointed out the guarantee that they must continue to do these things, and to do them more and more thoroughly, if they would not lose their place in the crowd of States, and be finally vanquished and overthrown . . .

FRIEDRICH VON GENTZ

THE TRUE CONCEPT OF A BALANCE OF
POWER (1806). *Extract*

[From: *Fragmente aus der neusten Geschichte des Politischen Gleichgewichts in
Europa.* Zweite Auflage. St Petersburg 1806. Chapter 1, pp. 1–10. Translated by Dr Patricia M. Sherwood.]

Friedrich von Gentz (1764–1832) was a Prussian diplomat and
publicist who vigorously opposed both the French Revolution and
Napoleonic expansionism. From 1810 he was closely associated with
Metternich and was Secretary-General of the Congress of Vienna.
His *Fragmente auz der neusten Geschichte des politischen Gleichgewichts in
Europa* (1806), which was immediately translated into English, was
both an anti-Napoleonic tract and an outline of the basic principles
underlying the eventual post-war settlement. A notable feature of his
exposition of classical balance-of-power theory is the analogy which
he draws with a civil or domestic constitution, enabling him to
justify a similarly aristocratic or hierarchical structure in the 'international association'.

What is usually termed a *balance of power* is that constitution
which exists among neighbouring states more or less connected
with each other, by virtue of which none of them can violate the
independence or the essential rights of another without effective
resistance from some quarter and consequent danger to itself.

Many misconceptions have arisen as a result of the simi-
larity with physical objects upon which the term was based. It
has been supposed that those who saw in the *balance of power*
the basis of an association of states were aiming at the most
complete *equality*, or *equalization*, of power possible, and were
demanding that the various states of an area which is politically united should be most precisely measured, weighed and
rounded off, one against the other, in respect of size, population, wealth, resources, etc. This false assumption, upon being
applied to state relations with either credulity or scepticism,
has led to two opposite errors, one almost as damaging as the
other. Those who fully accepted this imaginary principle were
led to believe that in every case where one state became

stronger, either through external growth or internal development, the others would offer resistance and would feel obliged to struggle until they had either matched this increase in strength or reduced the state to its former condition. But, on the other hand, others, in their quite correct conviction that such a system is impossible, have called the whole idea of a balance of power a chimera, invented by dreamers and skilfully manipulated by artful men so that there should be no lack of pretexts for dispute, injustice and violence. The former of these errors would banish peace from the earth; the latter would offer the most desirable prospects of absolute power to any state thirsting for conquest.

Both errors are based on the same confusion of ideas to which, in the field of internal state relations, we owe all the frivolous and airy theories of *civil equality* and all the unsuccessful practical attempts to carry them out. All the citizens in every well-ordered state, and all the states in every well-ordered community of nations, should be *equal in law* or *equal before the law*, but by no means *equal in rights*. True equality, the only kind attainable by legitimate means, consists in both cases only in this, that the smallest as well as the greatest is assured of his right, and cannot be compelled or harmed by unlawful authority.

The basis of a properly organized state and the triumph of its constitution is, namely, that a host of people, absolutely unequal in rights and power, in ability and its application, in inherited and acquired possessions, can exist alongside each other by means of common laws and government, that no-one can arbitrarily seize his neighbour's territory, and that the poorest man owns his cottage and his field as completely as the richest owns his palace and estates. Similarly, the true character of an international community (such as is being formed in modern Europe) and the triumph of its excellence will be that a certain number of states at very different levels of power and wealth, under the protection of a common bond, shall each remain unassailed within its own secure borders, and that he whose domain is bounded by a single town wall shall be held as inviolate by his neighbours as he whose possessions and authority extend over land and sea.

But as the best state constitution devised by man is never completely adequate for its purpose, and always leaves room for individual acts of violence, oppression and injustice, so the most perfect international constitution is never strong enough to prevent every attack of a stronger state on the rights of a weaker one. Furthermore, under otherwise identical conditions, an international association will always be less able to protect the independence and security of its members than a state will be to protect the legal equality and security of its citizens.

The security of the citizens of a state is based on the unity of its legislation and administration. The laws all emanate from the same central point; upholding them is the task of one and the same authority, which can dissuade those who would break the law by ordinary coercion at the outset, and bring those who have actually broken it to answer for it before a tribunal. The law binding states together lies only in their mutual treaties; and as these are open to endless variation in their essence, spirit and character because of the unlimited diversity of the relations from which they spring, so the nature of their origin excludes any higher, common sanction, in the strictest sense of the word. Among independent nations there is neither an executive nor a judicial power; to create the one, like the other, by means of external organizations has long been a fruitless pious wish and the vain endeavour of many a well-meaning man. But what the nature of the relation prevented from being achieved in its entirety was at least attained in approximation; and in the state system of modern Europe the problem was solved as happily as could be expected of men and the sensible application of human skill.

An extensive social union was formed among the states in this part of the world, of which the essential and characteristic aim was the preservation and mutual guarantee of the well-won rights of each of its members. From the time when this noble purpose was recognized in all its clarity there gradually developed also the vital and everlasting conditions on which its achievement depended. Men became aware that there were certain basic rules in the relationship between the strength of each individual part and the whole, without whose constant influence order could not be assured; and gradually the following maxims were established as a perpetual objective:

That if the state system of Europe is to exist and be maintained by common effort, no one of its members must ever become so powerful that the others cannot overcome it by joint action;

That if the system is not only to exist but also to be maintained without constant danger and violent concussions, then the other states must be capable of overcoming any individual who violates it, either by joint or majority action, if not by the action of a single state;

But that, in order to escape the alternative danger of an uninterrupted series of wars or arbitrary suppression of the weaker members in the short intervals of peace, the *fear* of common opposition or common vengeance by the others should normally be enough to keep each one in bounds; and

That if any European state attempted to attain power through unlawful activities, or had indeed attained it, so that it could defy the distant danger of an alliance between several of its neighbours, or the actual commencement of it, or even a federation of the whole, such a state should be treated as the common enemy of the whole community; if on the other hand such a power should appear somewhere on the stage through an accidental chain of events and through no illegal actions, no means of weakening it which the state has at its disposal should be left untried.

The essence of these maxims is the only generally understood theory of a balance of power in the political world.[1]

The original inequality of the parties in this type of association is not to be seen as an accidental circumstance, even less as an accidental evil, but to a certain extent as the precondition and foundation of the whole system;[2] not *how much power* one or the other possesses; but only whether he possesses it in such a way and under such limitations that he cannot with impunity deprive one of the rest of its own power—this is the question which must be decided in order to pass judgment at any given moment on the relation between individual parts or on the general proficiency of the edifice. Hence even a subsequent increase in that original necessary inequality may in itself be blameless, provided it does not come from sources, nor introduce incongruities, which violate one of the basic maxims.

Only when one or another state wilfully, or supported by fictitious pretexts and contrived titles, undertakes such acts which immediately or as an unavoidable consequence cause, on the one hand, the subjugation of its weaker neighbours and, on the other hand, perpetual danger, gradual debilitation and the final downfall of its stronger neighbours, only then, according to sound conceptions of the interest of a union of states, is a breakdown of the balance effected; only then do several states combine to prevent by means of an opportune counterweight the predominance of an individual state . . .

[1] It could perhaps more safely have been called a theory of *counterpoise*. For even the highest of its results is not so much a perfect *balance* as a constant *oscillation*, which can, however, never stray beyond certain limits because it is controlled by counterweights. (Gentz)

[2] If the world had been divided only into equal rectangles, large or small, no such union of states would ever have occurred, and the eternal war of each against the others would probably be the only world-event. (Gentz)

CHARLES MAURICE DE TALLEYRAND
LETTER TO METTERNICH

[From: *Mémoires, documents et écrits divers laissés par le Prince de Metternich*, ii. Paris 1880–4. pp. 524–9. Translated by John Warrington.]

Charles Maurice de Talleyrand (1754–1838) was a French statesman and diplomat whose career spanned the French Revolution, the Napoleonic period, the Restoration, and Louis Philippe's reign. Unprincipled and ambitious, Talleyrand nevertheless employed his considerable diplomatic skills on behalf of European equilibrium and peace. These objectives prompted him to a vain and costly attempt to restrain Napoleon in 1805, but the favour which he enjoyed with the Allies after Napoleon's defeat enabled him to play a prominent role at the Congress of Vienna, where he was France's representative. As this dispatch to Metternich shows, Talleyrand closely linked the idea of equilibrium with that of legitimacy, as Vergennes had associated it with justice.

Vienna, 19th December 1814

Your Highness,

I have hastened to fulfil the wishes of His Imperial and Apostolic Majesty [1] expressed in the letter with which Your Highness honoured me, and I have made known to His Most Christian Majesty [2] the confidential Note which you addressed on the 10th instant to the Chancellor of State, Prince von Hardenberg,[3] and which you have officially communicated to me.

To express the satisfaction that the King will derive from the resolutions set out in that Note, I need only to compare them with the instructions His Majesty gave his ambassadors to the Congress.

France had no ambitious project or personal interest to put forward there. Confined once more within her ancient boundaries, she had no dreams of extending them; like the sea, which never oversteps its shores except when stirred by storms, her armies, loaded with glory, aspire no longer to fresh conquests. Delivered from that aggression of which she had been less the instrument than the victim, happy to have had her legitimate princes restored and with them the repose she might have feared lost for ever, she had no objections to make, no claims that she desired to formulate. She has not raised and will never raise a single one. Nevertheless, she was still entitled to wish that the work of restoration should be accomplished for the whole of Europe as well as for herself, that everywhere and for ever the spirit of revolution should cease, that every legitimate right should be rendered sacred, and that every ambition or unjust enterprise should find condemnation and a permanent obstacle in an explicit acknowledgement and formal guarantee of those same principles of which the Revolution was nothing but a lethal disregard. The desire of France should be that of every European state which does not blind itself. Without such an order of things, none can for a moment feel certain of its future.

Never was a nobler purpose offered to the governments of Europe; never was a result so necessary, and never could its achievement be so confidently expected as at the moment when the whole of Christendom was summoned for the first time to form a Congress. It might perhaps already have been fully achieved if, as the King had hoped, the Congress at its initial meeting had, while laying down principles, decided the goal, and marked out the only road that could lead thereto. Then, without doubt, we should not have seen some Powers fashioning for themselves a pretext for the destruction of what could have nothing but preservation as its end. Indeed, when the treaty of 30th May expressed a wish that the final result of the deliberations of the Congress should be *real and lasting equilibrium*, it never intended to confound in one and the same mass all territories and all peoples in order then to divide them according to certain proportions; it wished that every legitimate dynasty should be either preserved or re-established, and that every legitimate right should be respected, and that vacant territories, meaning those without a sovereign, should be distributed conformably with the principles of political equilibrium, or, in other words, with those principles which tend to preserve the rights of each and the tranquillity of all. It would be, moreover, a very strange mistake to regard as unique elements of the equilibrium the quantities enumerated by political arithmeticians. 'Athens,' says Montesquieu, 'contained the same number of people both in the days of her splendid domination and in those of her shameful servitude. She had twenty thousand citizens when she defended the Greeks against the Persians, when she disputed the hegemony of Sparta, and when she attacked Sicily; she had twenty thousand when Demetrius of Phalerum counted them as slaves are counted in a market.' The equilibrium then will be a mere empty word if one takes account only of that ephemeral and deceptive strength produced by the passions and not of the true moral strength that consists in virtue. Now in the relations between one people and another the primary virtue is justice.

Imbued with these principles, the King laid down as an invariable rule to be followed by his ambassadors, that they should seek above all what is just and never disregard it in any circumstances whatever; that they should never subscribe to or acquiesce in anything contrary thereto, and that in the field of legitimate combinations, they should choose by preference those which can most effectively help towards the establishment and maintenance of a genuine equilibrium.

Of all questions down for discussion at the Congress, the King would have considered that of Poland as the first, the most important, the most pre-eminently European, beyond comparison with any other, had he been able to hope, as strongly as he desired it, that a people so worthy of the concern of all others, on account of its antiquity, its valour, the services it once rendered to Europe, and its subsequent misfortunes, would be restored to its ancient and unqualified independence. The partition which erased it from among the nations was the prelude to, in part the cause of, and perhaps to some extent the excuse for, these upheavals to which Europe has been prey. But when force of circumstances, carrying the day even against the noblest and most generous dispositions of the sovereigns to whom the formerly Polish provinces are subject, had reduced the Polish question to a simple matter of partition and boundaries, which the three interested Powers debated among themselves and from which their earlier treaties had excluded France, nothing remained for the latter, having offered to support the most equitable claims, but to hope you would be satisfied and to follow suit if you were. The question of Poland could no longer enjoy in the eyes of France, of Europe or in Poland itself, the pre-eminence it would have had on the assumption outlined above. The question of Saxony has now become the first and most important of all, because there is today no other in which the two principles of legitimacy and equilibrium have been compromised simultaneously and to such an extent as they have been by the arrangements proposed for that kingdom.

In order to acknowledge those arrangements as legitimate one would have to recognize as true the following propositions:

that Kings may be judged, and judged by anyone who wishes
and is able to seize their possessions; that they may be condemned without a hearing, without an opportunity to defend
themselves; that confiscation, removed from their legal codes
by all enlightened nations, should in the nineteenth century be
sanctioned by the general law of Europe, since confiscation of
a kingdom is undeniably less odious than that of a cottage;
that peoples have no rights distinct from those of their sovereigns, and can be likened to a small farmer's cattle; that
sovereignty is lost and acquired by the sole fact of conquest;
that the nations of Europe are not united among themselves by
moral ties other than those which unite them to the South Sea
islanders, that they live among themselves subject only to the
mere law of nature, and that what is called the public law of
Europe does not exist, on the supposition that, although civil
societies throughout the world are wholly or partially governed
by customs which for them are laws, the customs established
as between the nations of Europe, which have been universally,
continuously and reciprocally observed for three centuries,
are not a law for *them*; in a word that everything is lawful to
the strongest. But Europe, to whom these doctrines have done
so much harm, whom they have cost so many tears and so
much blood, has all too fully purchased the right to detest and
curse them. They inspire equal horror in Vienna, St Petersburg, London, Paris, Madrid, and Lisbon.

The arrangements proposed for the Kingdom of Saxony,
pernicious as an example, would be likewise in their effect
upon the general equilibrium of Europe, which consists in a
correspondence between the reciprocal forces of aggression and
defence of the various political bodies. Those arrangements
would damage it in two ways, both of them extremely serious:
1 By creating against Bohemia a very large aggressive force
and thus threatening the security of all Austria. For Bohemia's
own defensive force would have to be proportionately increased, at the expense of the defensive force of the Austrian
monarchy as a whole. Now the security of Austria means so
much to Europe that it cannot but arouse the King's particular solicitude.
2 By creating within the Germanic body, and for one of its

members, an aggressive force out of all proportion to the defensive force of all the others, a force which, by placing the latter in always imminent peril and obliging them to look elsewhere for support, would render ineffective the defensive force which, in the general system of European equilibrium, the body as a whole should offer but which it cannot possess except by the close union of its members.

France, like Austria, can say truthfully that she entertains no feelings of jealousy against Prussia; and it is precisely because of her genuine concern for Prussia that she cannot wish to see her gain apparent advantages, which, acquired by injustice and dangerous for Europe, would sooner or later prove lethal to Prussia herself. Let Prussia acquire all that she can lawfully obtain; France will not only refrain from opposing her, but will even be the first to applaud her. Let there be no more question of how much Saxon territory the King of Prussia [4] will cede to the King of Saxony [5]—a reversal of the whole idea of justice and reason. If, on the other hand, it is asked how much of Saxony her king will cede to the King of Prussia, and if, in order to secure more completely for Prussia an existence equal to that which she enjoyed in 1805, cessions are necessary on the part of the King of Saxony, the King of France will be the first to engage that prince to make such as are not calculated to threaten the interests of Austria and Germany, which constitute in this matter the general interests of Europe . . .

His Most Christian Majesty, being firmly resolved not to approve, even by his silence, the execution of projects formed against the King and Kingdom of Saxony, but liking to believe that those projects are the result of some error or illusion which a closer study will dispel; full of confidence too in the personal honesty and good feeling of His Majesty the King of Prussia, who also has experienced misfortune; knowing all that the influence of His Majesty the Emperor of all the Russians [6] can accomplish and all that can be rightly expected of all the fine qualities that distinguish him; convinced, finally, that one must never despair of a just cause, the King, I say, has not despaired of Saxony's. He will be still further from despair if he learns that His Majesty the Emperor of Austria, by a resolu-

tion worthy of himself, has nobly undertaken its defence and
declared that he will never abandon it.

[1] Emperor Francis I of Austria.
[2] Louis XVIII.
[3] The first Prussian plenipotentiary at the Congress of Vienna.
[4] Frederick William III.
[5] Frederick Augustus I.
[6] Alexander I.

CARL VON CLAUSEWITZ

ON WAR (1832). *Extract*

[From: *Vom Kriege*. Hinterlassenes Werk des Generals Carl von Clausewitz.
Sechzehnte Auflage. Bonn 1952. pp. 536–41. Translated by Dr Patricia M.
Sherwood.]

Carl von Clausewitz (1780–1831), a Prussian soldier and writer
who served in the Prussian Army during the Revolutionary and
Napoleonic wars, is best known as the author of *Vom Kriege*, a vast
treatise which has a central place in the history of strategic thought.
Less well known are the political sections, of which the following
extract is one of the most important. In this passage Clausewitz
employs a 'lattice' or 'network' metaphor in presenting an essentially
conservative notion of the balance of power.

. . . Finally we may further consider *allies* as the last support of
the defender. Of course we do not mean the usual allies, which
the attacker also has, but those who are *essentially concerned* with
the preservation of a country. For instance, if we look at the
republic of states of present-day Europe (without speaking of a
systematically regulated balance of power and interests, which
does not exist and has therefore often rightly been disputed),
we find it indisputable that the great and small interests of
states and peoples intersect each other in the most varied and
variable manner. Each such point of intersection creates a
binding knot, for in it the direction of the one is the counterweight to the direction of the other; obviously, through all

these knots a more or less great coherence of the whole is created, and this coherence must be partly weakened with every change. In this way the general relations of all states to one another serve rather to preserve the shape of the whole than to bring about changes in it, that is, there is this general *tendency*.

This, we believe, is how a balance of power should be understood, and in this sense it will happen spontaneously where several civilized states come into widespread contact.

How efficient this tendency of the general interests is in preserving the *status quo* is quite another thing ; certainly there are some changes in the relations of individual states with one another which can facilitate this efficiency of the whole, and others which can make it more difficult. In the first case they are efforts to improve the balance of power and since they have the same tendency as the general interests, then they will have the support of the majority of these interests. But in the other case they are deviations, overwhelming activity of single parts, true illnesses ; it is not to be wondered at that they appear in such a loosely bound whole as this quantity of large and small states, when they also appear in such a wonderfully ordered organic whole as that of all living nature.

If we are reminded, therefore, of instances in history where single states have been able to effect significant changes purely for their own benefit, without the whole even attempting to prevent it, or even of cases where a single state has found itself in a position to rise so far above the others that it became almost the absolute ruler of the whole, then our answer is this : this was no proof that the tendency of the general interests for the preservation of the *status quo* was not present, but only that its effectiveness at that moment was not great enough ; the striving towards a goal is something different from the movement towards it, but it is in no way futile, as we see to best advantage in the dynamics of the heavens.

We maintain that the tendency of the balance is the preservation of the *status quo*, assuming of course that repose, that is balance, was present in the *status quo* ; for where this has already been disturbed, tension arises and then the tendency of the balance can certainly lead to a change. But in the very nature of things this change can affect only a few single states, and never the majority. So it is certain that the latter see their preservation supported and ensured constantly, through the general interests of all—certain, too, that every single state which is not already in tension against the whole will have more interests in support of than in opposition to its defence.

Whoever dismisses these observations as a utopian dream does so at the expense of philosophical truth. Although this latter lets us see the relationships in which the essential elements of things stand to one another it would obviously be ill-considered to attempt, ignoring all accidental intervention, to deduce laws from it by which every single case could be regulated. But whoever, in the phrase of a great writer, *never rises above anecdote*, constructs all history on it, begins always with the most special thing, with the climax of the event, and goes down only as deep as there is reason to, and therefore never reaches the basically prevailing general relations, his opinion will never be of value for more than the one case, and that which philosophy has agreed upon for the generality of cases will seem like a dream to him.

If this general striving for tranquillity and preservation of the *status quo* were not present, then a number of civilized states could never exist alongside each other for any length of time without perforce fusing into one. Therefore, if Europe as it is today has lasted for over a thousand years, we can only ascribe this effect to the tendency of the general interests, and if the protection of the whole has not always sufficed to preserve each individual, these are irregularities in the life of the whole, which have however not destroyed it but been overcome by it.

It would be superfluous to go through the mass of events where changes which disturbed the balance too much have been prevented or reversed by the more or less open counter-action of the other states. Even the most fleeting glance at history will reveal them. We will mention only one case, because it is always on the lips of those who ridicule the idea of a balance of power, and because it seems particularly relevant here as a case in which a harmless defender succumbed without gaining any foreign support. We are speaking of Poland. That a state of eight million inhabitants could disappear, could be divided by three others, without any other state even drawing a sword seems at first glance to be a case which would either sufficiently prove the general ineffectiveness of the balance of power or at least show how far it can go in individual cases. That a state of such an extent could disappear and become a prize for others which were already among the most powerful (Russia and Austria) seemed an extreme case; and if such a case can rouse none of the general interests of the whole community of states, then it can be said that the effectiveness which these general interests should have for the preservation of individuals must be seen to be imaginary. But we maintain that even the most striking exception does not disprove the general rule, and we further maintain that the fall of Poland is not so incomprehensible as it may seem. Was Poland really to be considered a European state, a homogeneous member of the European republic of states? No! It was a Tartar state, which, instead of lying like the Crimean Tartars on the Black Sea, on the border of the European world, lay between the two on the Vistula. We are not speaking disparagingly of the people of Poland here, nor justifying the partition of the country, merely seeing things as they are. For a hundred years this state had basically played no further political role, but had merely become the bone of contention for others. It was impossible for it to last long amongst the others in its present condition and with its existing constitution; but any essential change in this Tartar state would have taken fifty or a hundred years, if the people's leaders had been in favour. But they were themselves too Tartar to desire such a change. Their disorganized political life and immeasurable frivolity went hand in hand and so they tumbled into the abyss. Long before the partition of Poland the Russians were as good as at home there, and the conception of an independent, separate state had disappeared; nothing was more certain than that Poland, if it were not divided, would become a province of Russia. If all this had not been so, and Poland had been a state capable of defence, the three Powers would not have moved towards its partition so easily, and those Powers most concerned with its preservation, such as France, Sweden and Turkey, would have been able to co-operate quite differently to preserve it. But if a state can only be preserved by outside help, then that is obviously asking too much.

The partition of Poland had often been talked of for over a hundred years, and since then the country had been seen not as a private house but as a public road on which foreign armies were constantly bustling. Were the other states to prevent all this, to keep their sword permanently drawn, in order to guard the political inviolability of the Polish border? That would have been to demand a moral impossibility. Poland was at this time politically little more than an uninhabited steppe; and little as one is able to protect for ever a defenceless steppeland, surrounded by other countries, from their invasions, in the same way one cannot guarantee the inviolability of this so-called state. For all these reasons one should wonder as little at the soundless downfall of Poland as at the quiet downfall of Crimean Tartary; in any case the Turks were more interested than any European state in the preservation of Poland, but they saw that it would be wasted effort to protect a defenceless steppe. . . .

RICHARD COBDEN

THE BALANCE OF POWER (1836). *Extract*

[From: *Political Writings*, i. 1868. pp. 256–69. Cobden's notes have been omitted.]

Richard Cobden (1804–1865) was a radical pamphleteer, politician and businessman. He travelled widely in Europe and America, and it was on his return from a tour of the Ottoman Empire, Egypt, and Greece that he published *Russia* (1836), which contains one of the severest denunciations of the balance of power. Its main interest lies in the detailed criticisms of earlier writers on the subject. Cobden tended to identify the balance of power with intervention in the affairs of other countries; he advocated the counter-doctrine of non-intervention, which he believed to be based on the principles of reason, justice and utility.

. . . The first instance in which we find the 'balance of power' alluded to in a king's speech, is on the occasion of the last address of William III to his parliament, December 31, 1701, where he concludes by saying—'I will only add this—if you do in good earnest desire to see England *hold the balance of Europe*, it will appear by your right improving the present opportunity.' From this period, down almost to our time (latterly, indeed, the phrase has become, like many other cant terms, nearly obsolete), there will be found, in almost every successive king's speech, a constant recurrence to the 'balance of Europe'; by which, we may rest assured, was always meant, however it might be concealed under pretended alarm for the 'equilibrium of power' or the 'safety of the Continent', the desire to see England 'hold the balance'. The phrase was found to please the public ear; it implied something of equity; whilst England, holding the balance of Europe in her hand, sounded like filling the office of Justice herself to one-half of the globe. Of course, such a post of honour could not be maintained, or its dignity asserted, without a proper attendance of guards and officers; and we consequently find that, at about this period of our history, large standing armies began to be called for; and not only were the supplies solicited by the government, from time to time, under the plea of preserving the liberties of Europe, but, in the annual mutiny bill (*the same in form as is now passed every year*), the preamble stated, amongst other motives, that the annual army was voted for the purpose of *preserving the balance of power in Europe*. The 'balance of power', then, becomes an important practical subject for investigation; it appeals directly to the business and bosoms of our readers, since it is implicated with an expenditure of more than a dozen millions of money per annum, every farthing of which goes, in the shape of taxation, from the pockets of the public.

Such of our readers as have not investigated this subject, will not be a little astonished to find a great discrepancy in the several definitions of what is actually meant by the 'balance of power'. The theory—for it has never yet been applied to practice—appears, after upwards of a century of acknowledged existence, to be less understood now than ever. Latterly, indeed, many intelligent and practical-minded politicians have thrown the question overboard, along with that of the balance of trade—of which number, without participating in their favoured attributes, we claim to be ranked as one. The

balance of power—which has, for a hundred years, been the
burden of kings' speeches, the theme of statesmen, the ground
of solemn treaties, and the cause of wars—which has served,
down to the very year in which we write, and which will, no
doubt continue to serve, for years to come, as a pretence for
maintaining enormous standing armaments, by land and sea,
at a cost of many hundreds of millions of treasure—the balance
of power is a chimera! It is not a fallacy, a mistake, an impos-
ture—it is an undescribed, indescribable, incomprehensible
nothing; mere words, conveying to the mind not ideas, but
sounds like those equally barren syllables which our ancestors
put together for the purpose of puzzling themselves about words,
in the shape of *Prester John*, or the *philosopher's stone*! We are bound,
however, to see what are the best definitions of this theory.

'By this balance,' says Vattel, 'is to be understood such a
disposition of things as that no one potentate or state shall be
able, absolutely, to predominate and prescribe laws to the
others.'—*Law of Nations*, b. 3, c. 3, § 47.

'What is usually termed a balance of power,' says Gentz, 'is
that constitution subsisting among neighbouring states, more
or less connected with one another, by virtue of which no one
among them can injure the independence or essential rights of
another without meeting with effectual resistance on some
side, and, consequently, exposing itself to danger.'—*Fragments on the Political Balance*, c. 1.

'The grand and distinguishing feature of the balancing
system,' says Brougham, 'is the perpetual attention to foreign
affairs which it inculcates; the constant watchfulness over
every nation which it prescribes; the subjection in which it
places all national passions and antipathies to the fine and
delicate view of remote expediency; the unceasing care which
it dictates of nations most remotely situated, and apparently
unconnected with ourselves; the general union which it has
effected of all the European powers, obeying certain laws, and
actuated in general by a common principle; in fine, the right
of mutual inspection, universally recognized, among civilized
states, in the rights of public envoys and residents.'—*Brougham's
Colonial Policy*, b. 3, § 1.

These are the best definitions we have been able to discover of the system denominated the balance of power. In the first place, it must be remarked that, taking any one of these descriptions separately, it is so vague as to impart no knowledge even of the writer's meaning; whilst, if taken together, one confuses and contradicts another—Gentz describing it to be 'a constitution subsisting among neighbouring states more or less connected with each other'; whilst Brougham defines it as 'dictating a care of nations most remotely situated, and apparently unconnected with ourselves'. Then it would really appear, from the laudatory tone applied to the system by Vattel, who says that it is 'such a disposition of things as that no one potentate or state *shall be able* absolutely to predominate and prescribe laws to the others'; as well as from the complacent manner in which Brougham states 'the general *union which it has effected* of all the European powers, obeying certain laws, and actuated in general by a common principle'—it would seem, from such assurances as these, that there was no necessity for that 'perpetual attention to foreign affairs', or that 'constant watchfulness over every nation', which the latter authority tells us, the system 'prescribes and inculcates'. The only point on which these writers, in common with many other authors and speakers in favour of the balance of power, agree, is in the fundamental delusion that such a system was ever acceded to by the nations of Europe. To judge from the assumption, by Brougham, of a 'general *union* among all the European powers'; from the allusion made by Gentz to that '*constitution* subsisting among neighbouring states'; or from Vattel's reference to 'a *disposition of things*', &c.—one might be justified in inferring that a kind of federal union had existed for the last century throughout Europe, in which the several kingdoms had found, like the States of America, uninterrupted peace and prosperity. But we should like to know at what period of history such a compact amongst the nations of the Continent was entered into? Was it previously to the peace of Utrecht? Was it antecedent to the Austrian war of succession? Was it prior to the seven years' war, or to the American war? Or did it exist during the French revolutionary wars? Nay, what period of the centuries during which Europe has (with only just sufficient intervals to enable the combatants to recruit their wasted energies) been one vast and continued battle-field, will Lord Brougham fix upon, to illustrate the salutary working of that 'balancing system' which 'places all national passions and antipathies in subjection to the fine and delicate view of remote expediency'?

Again, at what epoch did the nations of the Continent subscribe to that constitution, 'by virtue of which', according to Gentz, 'no one among them can injure the independence or essential rights of another'? Did this constitution exist, whilst Britain was spoiling the Dutch at the Cape, or in the East?—or when she dispossessed France of Canada?—or (worse outrage by far) did it exist when England violated the 'essential rights' of Spain, by taking forcible and felonious possession of a portion of her native soil? Had this constitution been subscribed by Russia, Prussia, and Austria, at the moment when they signed the partition of Poland?—or by France, when she amalgamated with a portion of Switzerland?—by Austria, at the acquisition of Lombardy?—by Russia, when dismembering Sweden, Turkey, and Persia?—or by Prussia, before incorporating Silesia?

So far from any such confederation having ever been, by written, verbal, or implied agreement, entered into by the 'European powers, obeying certain laws, and actuated in general by a common principle'; the theory of the balance of power has, we believe, generally been interpreted, by those who, from age to age, have, parrot-like, used the phrase, to be a system invented for the very purpose of supplying the want of such a combination. Regarding it for a moment in this point of view, we should still expect to find that the 'balancing system' had, at some period of modern history, been recognized and agreed to by all the Continental states; and that it had created a spirit of mutual concession and guarantee, by which the weaker and more powerful empires were placed upon a footing of equal security, and by which any one potentate or state was absolutely unable 'to predominate over the others'. But, instead of any such self-denial, we discover that the balance of Europe has merely meant (if it has had a meaning) that which our blunt Dutch king openly avowed as his aim to his parliament—a desire, on the part of the great powers, to '*hold the balance of Europe*'. England has, for nearly a century, held the European scales—not with the blindness of the goddess of justice herself, or with a view to the equilibrium of opposite interests, but with a Cyclopean eye to her own aggrandizement. The same lust of conquest has actuated, up to the measure of their abilities, the other great powers; and, if we find the smaller states still, in the majority of instances, preserving their independent existence, it is owing, not to the watchful guardianship of the 'balancing system', but to the limits which nature herself has set to the undue extension of territorial dominion—not only by the physical boundaries of different countries, but in those still more formidable moral impediments to the invader—the unity of language, laws, customs, and traditions; the instinct of patriotism and freedom; the hereditary rights of rulers; and, though last not least, that homage to the restraints of justice which nations and public bodies have in all ages avowed, however they may have found excuses for evading it.

So far, then, as we can understand the subject, the theory of a balance of power is a mere chimera—a creation of the politician's brain—a phantasm, without definite form or tangible existence—a mere conjunction of syllables, forming words which convey sound without meaning. Yet these words have been echoed by the greatest orators and statesmen of England: they gingled successively from the lips of Bolingbroke, Chatham, Pitt, Burke, Fox, Sheridan, Grey, and Brougham;—ay, even whilst we were in the act of stripping the maritime nations of the Continent of their colonies, then regarded as the sole source of commercial greatness; whilst we stood sword in hand upon the neck of Spain, or planted our standard on the rock of Malta; and even when England usurped the dominion of the ocean, and attempted to extend the sphere of human despotism over another element, by insolently putting barriers upon that highway of nations—even then, the tongues of our orators resounded most loudly with the praises of the 'balance of power'! There would be something peculiarly humiliating in connection with this subject, in beholding the greatest minds of successive ages, instead of exercising the faculty of thought, become the mere automata of authority, and retail, with less examination than the haberdasher bestows upon the length, breadth, and quality of his wares, the sentiments bequeathed from former generations of writers and speakers—but that, unhappily, the annals of philosophy and of past religions, afford too many examples of the triumph of mere imitativeness over the higher faculties of the human intellect.

We must not, however, pass over the 'balance of power', without at least endeavouring to discover the meaning of a phrase which still enters into the preamble of an annual act of Parliament, for raising and maintaining a standing army of ninety thousand men. The theory, according to the historian Robertson, was first invented by the Machiavellian statesmen of Italy during the prosperous era of the Florentine (miscalled) republic; and it was imported into Western Europe in the early part of the sixteenth century, and became 'fashionable', to use the very word of the historian of Charles V, along with many other modes borrowed, about the same time, from that commercial and civilized people. This explanation of its origin does not meet with the concurrence of some other writers; for it is singular, but still consistent with the ignis-fatuus character of the 'balance of power', that scarcely two authors agree, either as to the nature or the precise period of invention of the system. Lord Brougham claims for the theory an origin as remote as the time of the Athenians; and Hume describes Demosthenes to have been the first advocate of the 'balancing system'—very recommendatory, remembering that ancient history is little else than a calendar of savage wars! There can be little doubt, however, that the idea, by whomsoever or at whatever epoch conceived, sprang from that first instinct of our nature, fear, and originally meant at least some scheme for preventing the dangerous growth of the power of any particular state; *that power being always regarded, be it well remembered, as solely the offspring of conquest and aggrandizement:* notwithstanding, as we have had occasion to show in a former page of this pamphlet, in the case of England and the United States, that labour, improvements, and discoveries, confer the greatest strength upon a people; and that, by these alone, and not by the sword of the conqueror, can nations, in modern and all future times, hope to rise to supreme power and grandeur. And it must be obvious that a system professing to observe a 'balance of power'—by which, says Vattel, 'no one potentate or state shall be able absolutely to predominate'; or, according to Gentz, 'to injure the independence or essential rights of another'; by which, says Brougham, 'a perpetual attention to foreign affairs is inculcated, and a constant watchfulness over every nation is prescribed':—it must be obvious that such a 'balancing system'—if it disregards those swiftest strides towards power which are making by nations excelling in mechanical and chemical science, industry, education, morality, and freedom—must be altogether chimerical.

Lord Bacon, indeed, took a broader and more comprehensive view of this question when he wrote, in his essay on empire—'*First*, for their neighbours, there can no general rule be given (the occasions are so variable) save one, which ever holdeth; which is, that princes do keep due sentinel, that none of their neighbours do overgrow so (by increase of territory, by *embracing of trade*, by approaches, *or the like*), as they become more able to annoy them than they were: and this is generally the work of standing councils, to see and *to hinder it*.' This appears to us to be the only sound and correct view of such a principle as is generally understood by the phrase, 'the balance of power'. It involves, however, such a dereliction of justice, and utter absence of conscientiousness, that subsequent writers upon the subject have not dared to follow out the principle of hindering the growth of trade, and the like (which includes all advance in civilization); although, to treat it in any other manner than that in which it is handled by this 'wisest, greatest, meanest of mankind', is to abandon the whole system to contempt, as unsound, insufficient, and illusory. As for the *rule* of Lord Bacon; were the great Enemy of mankind himself to summon a council, to devise a law of nations which should convert this fair earth, with all its capacity for life, enjoyment, and goodness, into one vast theatre of death and misery, more dismal than his own dark Pandemonium, the very words of the philosopher would compose that law! It would reduce us even below the level of the brute animals. *They* do not make war against their own instincts; but this 'rule' would, if acted upon universally, plunge us into a war of annihilation with that instinct of progression which is the distinguishing nature of intellectual man. It would forbid all increase in knowledge, which, by the great writer's own authority, is power. It would interdict the growth of morality and freedom, which are power. Were Lord Bacon's 'rule' enforced, not only would the uninstructed Russians commence a crusade against our steam-engines and our skilful artisans; the still more barbarous Turk would be called upon to destroy the civilization and commerce of Petersburgh; the savage African would be warranted, nay, compelled to reduce the turbaned Osmanli to his own nakedness and a wigwam; nor would the levelling strife cease until either the '*rule*' were abrogated, or mankind had been reduced to the only pristine possessions—teeth and nails!

The balance of power, then, might, in the first place, be very well dismissed as *chimera*, because no state of things, such as the 'disposition', 'constitution', or 'union', of European powers, referred to as the basis of their system, by Vattel, Gentz, and Brougham, ever did exist;—and, secondly, the theory could, on other grounds, be discarded as *fallacious*, since it gives no definition—whether by breadth of territory, number of inhabitants, or extent of wealth—according to which, in balancing the respective powers, each state shall be estimated; —whilst, lastly, it would be altogether incomplete and inoperative, from neglecting, or refusing to provide against, the silent and peaceful aggrandizements which spring from improvement and labour. Upon these triple grounds, the question of the balance of power might be dismissed from further consideration. . . .

The Armed Peace

HENRY REEVE

BALANCE OF POWER (1875). *Extract*

[From: *Encyclopaedia Britannica*, iii. 9th edition, 1875. pp. 267–8, 271–2.]

Henry Reeve (1813–1895) was on the staff of *The Times* for fifteen years and editor of the *Edinburgh Review* for forty years. Lord Strang describes him as 'the intimate of statesmen and diplomatists at home and abroad—an eminent Victorian'. In his article on the balance of power for the *Encyclopaedia Britannica* (9th ed. 1875), Reeve criticizes the idea from essentially the same standpoint as Cobden, but he ends by calling for 'a truer balance of power' based on 'sounder principles'.

The theory of the Balance of Power may be said to have exercised a preponderating influence over the policy of European statesmen for more than two hundred years, that is, from the Treaty of Westphalia until the middle of the present century; and to have been the principal element in the political combinations, negotiations, and wars which marked that long and eventful period of modern history. It deserves, therefore, the attentive consideration of the historical student, and, indeed, the motive cause of many of the greatest occurrences would be unintelligible without a due estimate of its effects. Even down to our own times it has not been without an important influence; for the Crimean War of 1854 was undertaken by England and France for no other object than to maintain the balance of power in Eastern Europe, and to prevent the aggrandizement of Russia by the dismemberment of the Ottoman empire and the conquest of Constantinople. Nevertheless there is, perhaps, no principle of political science, long and universally accepted by the wisest statesmen, on which modern opinion has, within the last twenty years, undergone a greater change; and this change of opinion is not merely speculative, it has regulated and controlled the policy of the most powerful states, and of none more than of Great Britain, in her dealings with the continent of Europe. At the date of the publication of the last edition of this work, the theory of the balance of power was believed to be so firmly established, both by reason and experience, that it was laid down, in the forcible words of Earl Grey, that 'the poorest peasant in England is interested in the balance of power, and that this country ought to interfere whenever that balance appeared to be really in danger'. At the present time no English statesman would lay down that proposition categorically; and probably no European statesman would be prepared to act upon it. In proportion as the theory of the balance of power has lost much of its former authority, the doctrine of non-intervention has gained strength and influence, and this has been accepted at the present day both by Whig and Tory ministers, so that no strong difference of opinion can at the present time be said to exist in the British nation on the subject. Within the last fifteen years political changes of extraordinary magnitude have been brought about in Europe by force of arms and by revolutions. In former times such changes would certainly have led to a general war, on the principle that it was essential to maintain the relative strength and independence of states, and to support the fabric of European policy. But, under the policy of non-intervention, the effects of these contests have been confined to the states which were directly engaged in them; and the other powers of Europe have maintained a cautious neutrality, which has probably not lessened their own strength, and which has saved the world from a general conflagration.

The theory of the balance of power rested on several assumptions. It was held, more especially from the time of Grotius, in the early part of the seventeenth century, that the states of Europe formed one grand community or federal league, of which the fundamental principle and condition was the preservation of the balance of power; that by this balance (in the words of Vattel) was to be understood such a disposition of things, as that no one potentate or state shall be able absolutely to predominate and prescribe laws to the others; that all were equally interested in maintaining this common settlement, and that it was the interest, the right, and the duty of

every power to interfere, even by force of arms, when any of
the conditions of this settlement were infringed or assailed by
any other member of the community. The principle can hardly
be more tersely expressed than in the words of Polybius (lib. i.
cap. 83): 'Neque enim ejusmodi principia contemnere
oportet, neque tanta cuiquam astruenda est potentia, ut cum
eo postea de tuo quamvis manifesto jure disceptare ex æquo
non queas.'[1] Or, to borrow the language of Fénelon in his
Instructions, drawn up by him for the guidance of the Duc de
Bourgogne, 'This attention to maintain a sort of equality and
equipoise between neighbouring nations is the security of the
general tranquillity. In this respect all neighbouring nations,
trading with each other, form one great body and a sort of
community. Thus, Christendom is a kind of universal republic,
which has its interests, its fears, and its precautions to be taken.
All the members of this great body owe it to one another for the
common good, and owe it to themselves for the security of their
country, to prevent the progress of any other members who
should seek to overthrow this balance, which would turn to
the certain ruin of all the other members of the same body.
Whatever changes or affects this general system of Europe is
too dangerous, and draws after it infinite mischiefs.' Whatever
may be the value of these philanthropic principles, history
reminds us that when they were most loudly professed they
were most frequently violated, and that no cause of war seems
to have been so frequent or so fatal as the spurious pretext of
restoring peace and defending the general tranquillity of the
world. Thus, it was to balance the power of the house of
Austria that Cardinal Richelieu flung France into the quarrels
of Germany in the Thirty Years' War, and even lent her aid to
the Protestant cause. It was to balance the encroaching and
aggressive power of Louis XIV that numerous combinations
were formed between England, Austria, and Holland, which,
after nearly half a century of almost uninterrupted contests
and bloodshed, ended in the peace of Utrecht. The pretext of
Frederick II, when he was meditating some act of rapine,
generally was that he believed some hostile combination had
been formed against him, which it was wise to anticipate. In
short, no cause of war has been more frequently alleged and

acted upon, than that a proper consideration for the balance
of power rendered it necessary to take forcible measures to
avert some remote or hypothetical danger.

It is obviously a maxim, not only of policy but of common
sense and human nature, that the weak should combine to
protect themselves against the strong, and that when the
independence of minor states is threatened by the ambition or
the overwhelming superiority of a power aiming at universal
empire, they will do wisely to unite for the purposes of self-
defence and resistance. Frederick II himself says, in his *Anti-
Machiavel*, where he laid down precepts which he did not
practise, 'When the excessive aggrandizement of one power
threatens to overwhelm all others, it is the part of wisdom to
oppose barriers to its encroachments, whilst there is yet time to
stay the torrent. The clouds are seen to gather, the lightning
announces a coming storm, and the sovereign who is unable to
contend against the tempest will, if he is wise, unite himself
with all those who are menaced by the same common danger.
Had the kings of Egypt, Syria, and Macedonia confederated
together against the Roman power, they would not have fallen
under its oppressive yoke; an alliance prudently contracted,
and a war carried on with energy, would have saved the
ancient world from universal despotism.' So too, Hume, in his
celebrated *Essay on the Balance of Power*, endeavours to show
that the ancients were familiar with the principle both as
statesmen and historians, and, for example, he avers that whoever will read Demosthenes's oration for the Megalopolitans,
will see the utmost refinements on this principle that ever
entered into the head of a Venetian or European speculatist.

But with great respect to these illustrious authorities, they
appear to have discussed, under the name of the balance of
power, a principle which might more fitly be termed a theory
of warlike alliances. The object of the balance of power, rightly
understood, is not to carry on war with success, but to avoid
war altogether, by establishing a common interest and obligation in the maintenance of the conditions of peace. When war
is declared, public law is suspended, and each state must be
guided by what it conceives to be its own interest and duty. If
the theory of the balance of power has any value at all, it is not

in the hour of violence and bloodshed, when the fate of nations may be decided on a field of battle, but rather in those negotiations which must eventually terminate the contest, which commonly bring together for that purpose the representatives of all the belligerents, and which are designed to provide against the recurrence of these calamities.

The ablest and most eloquent champion of the system of equipoise in the present century was the Chevalier von Gentz, who published his *Fragments upon the Balance of Power in Europe* in 1806, under the influence of the catastrophe which had subjugated the Continent, and who subsequently took an active part at the Congress of Vienna in the attempts to constitute a new system of European policy. Gentz defines the balance of power as 'a constitution subsisting between neighbouring states more or less connected with one another, by virtue of which no one among them can injure the independence or essential rights of another, without meeting with effectual resistance on some side, and consequently exposing itself to danger.' And he rests this constitution on four propositions:—1. That no state must ever become so powerful as to coerce all the rest; 2. That every state which infringes the conditions is liable to be coerced by the others; 3. That the fear of coercion should keep all within the bounds of moderation; and 4. That a state having attained a degree of power to defy the union should be treated as a common enemy. He argues that by a strict adherence to these principles wars would be averted, excessive power restrained, and the independent existence of the humblest members of the confederacy secured. But, for the reasons we have previously assigned, it is a fallacy to suppose that even the civilized states of Europe have ever naturally formed a confederacy, or that their relations are governed by common rules of action, recognized alike by all of them. That theory supplies a very insecure basis for the balance of power and the maintenance of peace. The law of nations, not being imposed or sanctioned by any supreme and sovereign authority, is, in fact, reducible to the general laws of morality, which ought to regulate the dealings of mankind, except when it has been expressed and established in the form of a contract, binding on all the parties to that obligation. To determine the true character and limits of the balance of power, we must have recourse, not to vague general principles, but to positive law, framed in the shape of international contracts, which are termed treaties, and which have been sanctioned at different epochs of modern history by a congress of states. This historical treatment of the subject leads us to more tangible and solid ground; and it will be seen that on these occasions more especially attempts have been made to establish a balance of power in Europe upon the basis of general treaties; and that these attempts have been rewarded by considerable, though not by permanent, success in the seventeenth, eighteenth, and nineteenth centuries. . . .

. . . The balance of power, as it was understood fifty years ago, and down to a more recent time, has been totally destroyed; no alliances can be said to exist between any of the great powers, but each of them follows a distinct course of policy, free from any engagements to the rest, except on some isolated points; the minor states can appeal to no certain engagement or fixed general principle for protection, except, perhaps, as far as the neutrality of Switzerland and Belgium is concerned; and for the last two centuries there has not been a time at which all confidence in public engagements and common principles of international law has been so grievously shaken. Where the reign of law ends, the reign of force begins, and we trace the inevitable consequence of this dissolution of legal international ties in the enormous augmentation of military establishments, which is the curse and the disgrace of the present age. Every state appears to feel that its security depends on arming the whole virile population, and maintaining in what is called a state of peace all the burdens of a complete armament; indeed, in the most barbarous ages and the most sanguinary wars there were, doubtless, fewer men under arms, and less money was spent in arming them, than at the present day.

We have shown in the preceding observations that we do not retain the faith of our forefathers in the balance of power. It is impossible to equalize the strength of nations. It is impossible to regulate or control the growth and development of their forces, which depend not on territorial possessions alone, but on their industry, their credit, their natural resources, and their internal institutions. It is impossible to weigh their relative power and influence in nice or golden scales, nor can we always compel them 'parcere subjectis et debellare superbos'.[2] But the recognition of certain mutual obligations and principles of public law is the fundamental condition of civilization itself. Nothing can be more injurious to society than that the states of Europe should exist without alliances, without mutual confidence, without a common system based on the principles of justice and of peace, the weak living in dread of the strong, the strong armed to the teeth against each other. We trust that before another great catastrophe arises from this state of disguised hostility, a truer balance of power may be established by a return to sounder principles; for peace can never be secure unless it is protected by the concurrence of the leading nations of the world, and by their determination to oppose a combined resistance to those who have no object but their own aggrandizement and ambition.

[1] 'No contribution should be made to the acquisition by any one state of such great power that dispute with her is impossible, even where the claim is agreed to be just.'

[2] 'to spare the conquered and crush the proud' (Vergil, *Aeneid* vi, 853).

SIR EDWARD GREY

MINUTES OF THE COMMITTEE OF IMPERIAL DEFENCE AT A MEETING OF 26th MAY 1911. *Extract*

[From: *British Documents on the Origins of the War 1898–1914*, vi. Ed. G. P. Gooch and Harold Temperley. H.M.S.O. 1930. pp. 782–4.]

Sir Edward Grey (1862–1933) was Foreign Secretary from December 1905 to May 1916, the longest continuous tenure of that office. In the years between the two Moroccan crises Grey became increasingly preoccupied with the divisions in Europe. In this 1911 speech to the Imperial Defence Committee he refers to the possibility of a 'Napoleonic policy' on the part of 'the strongest power in Europe, or of the strongest group of Powers in Europe'. Grey stresses the 'free hand' traditionally associated with Britain's balancing role.

. . . Of course it is difficult to deal with Foreign Policy as a whole. It is not like something which can be put into a Bill, or even expressed in a Resolution. It must necessarily be rather vague, but I will try and make it as definite as I can. To explain what the present situation is as between ourselves and other Powers in Europe, I think I must go back a little into history, because we cannot understand the present situation without knowing how we came to arrive at it. I must go back rather an alarming way to the time when I first became Under-Secretary at the Foreign Office in 1892; but though it sounds rather alarming to go back as far as that, it will not take very long to explain what the situation was then, and then to jump from that to the present moment. In 1892 the situation then, and for some years previously, had been this: that the two restless Powers in Europe were France and Russia; that is, they were the two Powers from whom trouble to the peace of Europe was expected, if at all. The solid quiet group in Europe at that time was the Triple Alliance of Germany, Austria, and Italy. It had been the policy of Lord Salisbury before 1892, and it was the policy of Mr Gladstone's Government of 1892, not to join the Triple Alliance or come under definite commitment to it, but generally in diplomacy to side with the Triple Alliance as being the stable Power in Europe, and the one which was securing the peace. Therefore, because the Triple Alliance was the stable Power while France and Russia were supposed to be the restless Powers, which might trouble the peace, the weight of British influence and diplomacy was thrown, when required, quietly and unostentatiously, and not aggressively, but decidedly into the scale on the side of the Triple Alliance. Soon after 1892 the situation began slowly to change. It was never, perhaps, a very agreeable situation. During the whole of that time we were not by any means on the best of terms with Germany. We were constantly having— though we were siding with the Triple Alliance—friction about African questions—friction about questions in China, but the situation was not in the least alarming—there was no question of a breach of the peace, or the rupture of diplomatic relations —but there was constant friction. It was not very comfortable, even so far as Germany was concerned; but as regards Russia and France, the situation was very much worse. The diplomatic atmosphere between ourselves and Russia and France in

those years was such that the least incident in any part of the
world, whether the Russian seizure of Port Arthur, the Russian
action on the Pamirs on the Indian frontier, or French action
in Siam—the least incident of that kind—at once excited the
press of both countries, and there were rumours of wars more
than once. I know it was thought at one time that we were on
the verge of war with France over Siam; for instance in 1893—
I do not think it was ever really true, but it was bad enough
that it should ever be thought so, and everybody knows the
scares there were of war with Russia from time to time. We
wanted peace. We did not want that sort of thing to go on, and
the late Government, I imagine—I was not of course a
member of it—got tired of the situation, and said, 'Now after
all, what are these troubles with France? Egypt is an old story;
Siam really not a matter which two great nations ought to
quarrel about—all these things between us and France surely
are things which, if the diplomatic atmosphere could be made
better, would cause no trouble really to the Governments of the
two countries.'

After discussions lasting a long time, the result was the
Anglo-French Agreement of 1904. This agreement at once
removed all risk of a quarrel between the United Kingdom
and France, and by removing that, brought the two nations
very rapidly to realize that there were no causes of quarrel
which ought to divide them, and that there was no reason
why they should not be the best of friends. So far, again, that
was all to the good. Then, since we have been in office, after the
bitterness of the Russo-Japanese war had disappeared, the
same policy was pursued with Russia. I do not really think
that Russia ever had designs on the Indian frontier for the
invasion of India. Some military people in Russia may have
had their private opinion about that, but I do not believe the
Russian Government ever seriously had designs for invading
India. But in any case it was thought that she had. After the
Russo-Japanese war it became possible to talk over some of
those questions with Russia, especially the question of Persia,
which I will come to later on, and both countries convinced
themselves, we, that Russia would cease to prosecute railways
and so forth towards the Indian frontier, which might be dis-

turbing to us; while she became convinced that we would not undermine her position in the north of Persia, and would not work against her in diplomatic matters in Europe. So that cause of quarrel disappeared, and, consequently, we and Russia have now become very good friends in diplomacy. That was all to the good. But nothing in these affairs is entirely to the good. As our relations with Russia and France improved, it became apparent that our relations with Russia and France were better than our relations with Germany were. The press, both in Germany and here, began to pay more attention to the differences between Germany and us. I think there was considerable jealousy in public circles in Germany that we should have put ourselves on such good relations with Russia and France. Germany could never profit by any difference between us and them, as she had undoubtedly done in previous years, and the result was generally that the diplomatic atmosphere as regards Germany was not so good as it was before. At the present moment the German and British Governments are not having difficulties with each other. The questions which we have to discuss we discuss frankly, and the difficulties are not between the two Governments. We are most anxious to keep on the best of terms with Germany. I believe she is also genuinely anxious to be on good terms with us, and we smooth over the matters which arise between us without difficulty. There is, for instance, the question of war claims,—General Botha may be surprised to hear that Germany is still making claims upon us for compensation arising out of those unhappy days which have now passed so far away from us. Questions of that kind are going on, and the two Governments do smooth them over, but we must make it a cardinal condition in all our negotiations with Germany that if we come to any understanding with Germany of a public kind which puts us on good relations with Germany it must be an understanding which must not put us back into the old bad relations with France and Russia. That means to say that if we publicly make friendship with Germany it must be a friendship in which we take our existing friends in Europe with us, and to which they become parties, so that if to the world at large it is demonstrated that it is quite clear there is as little chance of there being a disturbance of the peace between us and Germany as there is at the present moment of there being a disturbance of the peace between us and France, or us and Russia, it must also be clear that, side by side with that, it will become equally apparent that there is no chance of a disturbance of the peace between Germany and France or Germany and Russia. That is what I mean by taking our friends with us into any new friendship into which we may go. Why I lay stress on that is this: There is no danger, no appreciable danger, of our being involved in any considerable trouble in Europe, unless there is some Power, or group of Powers, in Europe which has the ambition of achieving what I would call the Napoleonic policy. That would be a policy on the part of the strongest Power in Europe, or of the strongest group of Powers in Europe, of first of all separating the other Powers outside their own group from each other, taking them in detail, crushing them singly if need be, and forcing each into the orbit of the policy of the strongest Power, or of the strongest group of Powers. Now, if any policy of that sort was pursued by any Power, it could only be pursued by the strongest Power, or the strongest group of Powers in Europe at the moment. The moment it was pursued, the moment the weakest Powers in Europe were assailed, either by diplomacy or by force, one by one they would appeal to us to help them. I may say at once we are not committed by entanglements which tie our hands. Our hands are free, and I have nothing to disclose to our being bound by any alliances, which is not known to all the world at the present time. But I do feel this very strongly, that if such a situation should arise, and there was a risk of all the Powers, or a group of Powers, acquiring such a dominating position in Europe that on the Continent of Europe it would be the arbiter not only (of) peace and war, but of the diplomacy of all the other Powers of Europe, and if while that process was going on we were appealed to for help and sat by and looked on and did nothing, then people ought to realize that the result would be one great combination in Europe, outside which we should be left without a friend. If that was the result, then the naval situation would be this, that if we meant to keep the command of the sea we should have to estimate as a probable combination against us of fleets in Europe not two Powers but five Powers. Now, that is the situation, and that is why I say, though I do not think there is any prospect that one can reasonably see at the present moment of our being involved in serious trouble in Europe, it is possible that under such extreme conditions as I have named the question might arise as to whether we ought to take part by force in European affairs, and if we did it would be solely because Sea Power, and the necessity of keeping the command of the sea, was the underlying cause and motive of our action. So long as the maintenance of Sea Power and the maintenance and control of sea communication is the underlying motive of our policy in Europe, it is obvious how that is a common interest between us here at home and all the Dominions. . . .

LEWIS EINSTEIN

[From: 'The United States and Anglo-German Rivalry'. *National Review*, lx. January 1913. pp. 736–41.]

Lewis Einstein (1877–1967) served in diplomatic posts in London, Peking and Costa Rica before the First World War and as Secretary to the American Delegation at the important Algeciras Conference (First Moroccan Crisis) in 1906. His prescient article, 'The United States and Anglo-German Rivalry', found no publisher in America but appeared in England in the *National Review* early in 1913. In this essay he argued that the preservation of the European balance of power was essential to the national security of the United States and foreshadowed its eventual involvement in the First World War.

American life is still too intense, the problems of its economic development, and the relations between the individual and the State, still too unsettled, to have fostered an interest in the nation at large, in questions of foreign policy which are no less far-reaching in their nature, because not visibly oppressive. Yet the recent vast extension in foreign trade, and the gradual industrial evolution of the country, coupled with the growth of population, causing American exports to be increasingly manufactures, and decreasingly agricultural, must inevitably bring about an augmenting attention to questions of external order. Already, within the last decade, this has become noticeable in the importance which the so-called 'Open Door' in China, and the relations with Latin America have assumed before the public eye. In both instances, trade, present and future, has been the foundation and the objective of interest. The political cloak assumed, in the one case, by often repeated formulas regarding the integrity of China, in the other by the Monroe Doctrine and American sisterhood, has covered the very legitimate self-interest presented by the extension of commercial relations and the growth of the nation's influence.

Beyond this, however, watchfulness ceased. The affairs of Europe, picturesque and weighty as they appeared, yet seemed to have no immediate visible relation to the United States. In whatever direction might lie natural sympathies, the country as a whole remained unaware that its own interests were in any way concerned or affected by the future of the European problem and indifferent thereto. A traditional dis-interestedness continued as potent a formula of statecraft as half a century ago, without Americans realizing that altered conditions rendered necessary a modification of this attitude, and that the vast extension of international interests and the complexity of modern life no longer permitted former isola-tion. While the country had consciously altered its political, strategical and economic situation in the world by the creation of new oversea interests and the industrial growth of a century, it yet cherished the illusion of being able to preserve intact diplomatic ideas that had long since served their time. The belief prevailed that since in Europe, America had no terri-torial interests nor ambition, it had likewise no solicitude and could with impunity remain indifferent to whatever occurred on its political plane.

A brief retrospect suggests, however, ample proof to the contrary. The European balance of power has been such a permanent factor since the birth of the republic that Ameri-cans have never realized how its absence would have affected their political status. The national existence was first brought about by European dissension. When Pitt resisted Napoleon, the justifiable irritation felt against British high-handedness at sea caused Americans to forget that England's fight was in reality their own, and that the undisputed master of Europe would not have been long in finding pretexts to reacquire the Louisiana territory which, except for England, he would never have relinquished. When the Holy Alliance endeavoured to concentrate the power of Europe under the banner of legitimacy and divine right, Canning, by inspiring the Monroe Doctrine, interposed an effective restraint in the Western Hemisphere, and in the often-quoted phrase, 'called in the New World to redress the balance of the Old'.

Fifty years later, had England joined France in recognizing the Confederacy or in her abortive Mexican adventure, the history of the United States might have run a different course. At no time since the foundation of the Republic could a change materially altering the ancient European balance of power have been brought about without perceptibly affecting American interests and the position of the United States. Even to-day, in spite of the enormous increase in the country's resources and population, this political axiom holds as true as it did in the period of national formation and weakness. The undisputed paramountcy of any nation, both by land and sea, must inevitably make that Power a menace and a peril to every other country. In the words of a distinguished Secretary of State, Mr Olney, were the career of a Napoleon ever again to approach or even to threaten repetition, not merely sentiment and sympathy, but the strongest consideration of self-preservation and self-defence might compel the United States to take sides. It may therefore be of interest to survey the forces of war and peace to-day at work in Europe and see if there lies any menace to that balance of power, the preservation of which is essential to its national security.

At a time when arbitration and peace movements have assumed an unprecedented importance, it is a curious commentary on the age that there should likewise be so vast an increase of armaments and military preparation. The same scepticism in abstract justice, the same belief in the possible imminence of a great conflict, the same desire on the part of every nation to be the arbiter of its own political fortunes is apparent throughout the world. A feeling of unrest, moreover, has spread over Europe, and the inflammable state of its public opinion is everywhere noticeable. The modern conception of the nation in arms, and the prolonged situation of a a peace constantly more prepared for war is not the only cause for the existence of this spirit. The fresh taxation imposed by economically wasteful armaments at the same time as nations find themselves increasingly compelled to embark on extensive and expensive programmes of social reform, have contributed to augment the cost of life and the consequent dissatisfaction. There is, moreover, a growing discontent throughout Europe with the system of parliamentarism and certain results of representative Government. France, England, and Germany are all experiencing this, though for different causes and with different purposes in view. To a nation confronted by internal difficulties the diversion of an energetic foreign policy appealing to a united patriotism is always a possible alternative. That it has rarely been abused stands to the credit of European statesmanship. But in any survey of the existing situation, particularly on the Continent, it lurks in the background as a dangerous possibility.

It remains an anomaly that modern democratic government has been no more peaceful than former absolutism. Moltke's prophecy that popular rule enhanced the likelihood of war was correct. The situation lately witnessed in the parliamentary discussion over the Moroccan agreement in both Germany and France, where the leaders of political parties were far more combative and unyielding than their Government, proved significant, though in the one instance hostility was directed against England, while in the other it was against the readiness of the French Government to compromise. The high sensitiveness of a proud people, the confidence in its own strength, and the critical and often malignant scrutiny to which every Government is now exposed from within, are all factors contributing to embitter the atmosphere of international relations by stiffening the attitude of those in power.

Various elements have thus contributed to bring about the

present state of restlessness and uncertainty in Europe. Nor are
other signs wanting to confirm this. Like the flight of birds
before a storm, some indication of the belief in the likelihood of
an impending conflict may be gathered from the recent efforts
on the part of the smaller European States to preserve their
neutrality and their independence in the event of the greater
Powers going to war. Belgium, Holland, the Scandinavian
countries, and Switzerland, have each quite recently taken
stock of their position in such event, and embarked on fresh
military or naval programmes to increase the national security.
A wave of renewed militarism and nationalism has spread over
Europe. France, where it had lain dormant for years, is now
witnessing an intense revival provoked by the recent difficulties with Germany over Morocco, and excited by its
splendid success in aviation. In Russia the painful awakening
after the Manchurian War, has led to a reorganized Army and
the construction of a new Navy. In Austria-Hungary the
difficulties attending the late annexation prompted a military
reform, while gratitude to Germany for the assistance rendered
during that crisis, has led to an extensive battleship programme and awakened for the first time naval ambition. Italy
again, whatever be the future of her newly designed African
Empire, realizes that she has condemned herself during many
years to come to a vastly increased expenditure for armaments.

The sources of European unrest could, however, be more
lightly dismissed without the antagonism between Great
Britain and Germany. In spite of the attempts made on both
sides to explain it away, and to dwell on the pacific disposition
animating the construction of new 'Dreadnoughts', this
remains as an irreducible fact obscuring the political horizon.
Nor should it be regarded as a mere contest for commercial
supremacy on the part of two countries, one seeking to preserve, the other to gain new markets. Intelligent Germans are
the first to recognize that neither their merchants nor their
trade suffer in British Colonies. Beneath it lies the deeply
conscious rival ambition of two great nations, the one to
maintain undiminished the heritage conquered by its fore-
bears, the other to obtain the place 'under the sun' which it
regards as its right. And the magnitude of this issue is enhanced

by the hardly lesser constellations gravitating around the rivals, each with its own historic traditions and interests, but who have realized comparative security in a system which finds its political expression in the series of alliances and understandings forming the balance of modern Europe.

Paradoxical as it may seem, the grave danger of the present relations between Great Britain and Germany lies in the fact that there is no real difficulty between the two Powers. Where a concrete obstacle stands in the way, by compromise and mutual goodwill it may be removed. In recent years, the Anglo-French and Anglo-Russian negotiations, by a judicious policy of give-and-take, smoothed out through diplomatic means the colonial rivalry of a century. But between Germany and England similar adjustment is impossible. Their antagonism presents nothing concrete save rival ambition. Both Powers are logical and right in their attitude. From England's point of view she is carrying out her traditional policy of wellnigh four centuries. Whether set forth by an Elizabethan Cecil or a modern Lloyd George, whether directed against a Spanish Armada, the ambition of Louis XIV, the legions of Napoleon, or the might of William II, the purpose is the same. The same causes have made her the enemy of France and Russia, and the friend of Prussia, which make her to-day the friend of Russia and France and the adversary of a united Germany seeking oversea expansion.

The position of Germany is no less logical. Having achieved her unity and imperial position by blood and iron, there is no reason why she should abandon the element of armed force which has been the mainspring of her triumph. Patriotic Germans may differ among themselves whether an increased naval programme is advisable, but the nation is practically united with regard to the importance of maintaining her military supremacy, both by reason of an exposed central continental position and because of the unhealed wound inflicted on her Western neighbour. It is no fault of Germany if her strength is so huge that Europe trembles when she moves. Nor is she to blame if in the quest for new outlets all efforts at expansion under her own flag are thwarted by the Colonial Empires of her rivals. The unfortunate position of

Germany in this respect is readily apparent, but less obvious is
any peaceful remedy compatible with the interests of neutrals.
The suggestion lately advanced of compensation in the Congo,
or in the Portuguese Colonies, even if practicable would only
be a later cause of difficulty. It might delay, but could not
arrest, the growing antagonism between two great countries in
their struggle for supremacy. The appetite for Colonies is fed
on what it consumes, and a justifiable desire for more suitable
frontiers or enlarged boundaries would be the inevitable result
of such surrender. What on one side could be regarded as
generosity, would on the other be interpreted as weakness,
with the invitation for subsequent aggression brought about
by the pressure of strength. . . .

WINSTON CHURCHILL

[From: *The World Crisis 1911–1914*, 1923. pp. 11–14, 188–9.]

Winston Leonard Spencer Churchill (1874–1965), British statesman
and historian, had a varied career before the First World War as a
soldier, journalist, Member of Parliament, and cabinet minister. As
First Lord of the Admiralty from 1911 to 1915 he introduced many
valuable reforms, both administrative and technical, which contributed towards an efficient and prepared Navy on the eve of the war.
His account of these years in *The World Crisis* (vol. i, 1923), from
which the extract below is taken, combines a detailed narrative of
his role in the Government with a broad analysis of the 'world-wide
balance and combinations' of 'great States and Empires'.

. . . In the beginning of the twentieth century men were everywhere unconscious of the rate at which the world was growing.
It required the convulsion of the war to awaken the nations to
the knowledge of their strength. For a year after the war had
begun hardly anyone understood how terrific, how almost
inexhaustible were the resources in force, in substance, in
virtue, behind every one of the combatants. The vials of wrath
were full: but so were the reservoirs of power. From the end of

the Napoleonic Wars, and still more after 1870, the accumulation of wealth and health by every civilized community had been practically unchecked. Here and there a retarding episode had occurred. The waves had recoiled after advancing: but the mounting tides still flowed. And when the dread signal of Armageddon was made, mankind was found to be many times stronger in valour, in endurance, in brains, in science, in apparatus, in organization, not only than it had ever been before, but than even its most audacious optimists had dared to dream.

The Victorian Age was the age of accumulation; not of a mere piling up of material wealth, but of the growth and gathering in every land of all those elements and factors which go to make up the power of States. Education spread itself over the broad surface of the millions. Science had opened the limitless treasure-house of nature. Door after door had been unlocked. One dim mysterious gallery after another had been lighted up, explored, made free for all: and every gallery entered gave access to at least two more. Every morning when the world woke up, some new machinery had staited running. Every night while the world had supper, it was running still. It ran on while all men slept.

And the advance of the collective mind was at a similar pace. Disraeli said of the early years of the nineteenth century, 'In those days England was for a few—and for the very few.' Every year of Queen Victoria's reign saw those limits broken and extended. Every year brought in new thousands of people in private stations who thought about their own country and its story and its duties towards other countries, to the world and to the future, and understood the greatness of the responsibilities of which they were the heirs. Every year diffused a wider measure of material comfort among the higher ranks of labour. Substantial progress was made in mitigating the hard lot of the mass. Their health improved, their lives and the lives of their children were brightened, their stature grew, their securities against some of their gravest misfortunes were multiplied, their numbers greatly increased.

Thus when all the trumpets sounded, every class and rank had something to give to the need of the State. Some gave their science and some their wealth, some gave their business energy and drive, and some their wonderful personal prowess, and some their patient strength or patient weakness. But none gave more, or gave more readily, than the common man or woman who had nothing but a precarious week's wages between them and poverty, and owned little more than the slender equipment of a cottage, and the garments in which they stood upright. Their love and pride of country, their loyalty to the symbols with which they were familiar, their keen sense of right and wrong as they saw it, led them to outface and endure perils and ordeals the like of which men had not known on earth.

But these developments, these virtues, were no monopoly of any one nation. In every free country, great or small, the spirit of patriotism and nationality grew steadily; and in every country, bond or free, the organization and structure into which men were fitted by the laws, gathered and armed this sentiment. Far more than their vices, the virtues of nations ill-directed or mis-directed by their rulers, became the cause of their own undoing and of the general catastrophe. And these rulers, in Germany, Austria, and Italy; in France, Russia or Britain, how far were they to blame? Was there any man of real eminence and responsibility whose devil heart conceived and willed this awful thing? One rises from the study of the causes of the Great War with a prevailing sense of the defective control of individuals upon world fortunes. It has been well said, 'there is always more error than design in human affairs'. The limited minds even of the ablest men, their disputed authority, the climate of opinion in which they dwell, their transient and partial contributions to the mighty problem, that problem itself so far beyond their compass, so vast in scale and detail, so changing in its aspect—all this must surely be considered before the complete condemnation of the vanquished or the complete acquittal of the victors can be pronounced. Events also got on to certain lines, and no one could get them off again. Germany clanked obstinately, recklessly, awkwardly towards the crater and dragged us all in with her. But fierce resentments dwelt in France, and in Russia there were wheels within wheels. Could we in England perhaps by some effort, by some sacrifice of our material interests, by some compulsive gesture, at once of friendship and command, have reconciled France and Germany in time and formed that grand association on which alone the peace and glory of Europe would be safe? I cannot tell. I only know that we tried our best to steer our country through the gathering dangers of the armed peace without bringing her to war or others to war, and when these efforts failed, we drove through the tempest without bringing her to destruction . . .

. . . Like many others, I often summon up in my memory the impression of those July [1914] days. The world on the verge of its catastrophe was very brilliant. Nations and Empires crowned with princes and potentates rose majestically on every side, lapped in the accumulated treasures of the long peace. All were fitted and fastened—it seemed securely—into an immense cantilever. The two mighty European systems faced each other glittering and clanking in their panoply, but with a tranquil gaze. A polite, discreet, pacific, and on the whole sincere diplomacy spread its web of connections over both. A sentence in a despatch, an observation by an ambassador, a cryptic phrase in a Parliament seemed sufficient to adjust from day to day the balance of the prodigious structure. Words counted, and even whispers. A nod could be made to tell. Were we after all to achieve world security and universal peace by a marvellous system of combinations in equipoise and of armaments in equation, of checks and counter-checks on violent action ever more complex and more delicate? Would Europe thus marshalled, thus grouped, thus related, unite into one universal and glorious organism capable of receiving and enjoying in undreamed of abundance the bounty which nature and science stood hand in hand to give? The old world in its sunset was fair to see.

But there was a strange temper in the air. Unsatisfied by material prosperity the nations turned restlessly towards strife internal or external. National passions, unduly exalted in the decline of religion, burned beneath the surface of nearly every land with fierce, if shrouded, fires. Almost one might think the world wished to suffer. Certainly men were everywhere eager to dare. On all sides the military preparations, precautions and counter precautions had reached their height. France had her Three Years' military service; Russia her growing strategic Railways. The Ancient Empire of the Hapsburgs, newly smitten by the bombs of Sarajevo, was a prey to intolerable racial stresses and profound processes of decay. Italy faced Turkey; Turkey confronted Greece; Greece, Serbia and Roumania stood against Bulgaria. Britain was rent by faction and seemed almost negligible. America was three thousand miles away. Germany, her fifty million capital tax expended on munitions, her army increases completed, the Kiel Canal open for Dreadnought battleships that very month, looked fixedly upon the scene and her gaze became suddenly a glare. . . .

Statistical Chart of Europe (1804)

This anonymous chart is representative of the large statistica and comparative literature on the factors which were held to constitute the power of the various members of the European state-system. In its earliest form statistics (or 'political arithmetic') was the gathering and arrangement of information, usually numerical, about the political state. The relevance of this new branch of learning to the relations between states was soon recognized, and there were numerous writings in this vein, particularly between the 1780s and the 1830s. The method had its greatest practical success in the contributions of the Statistical Committee of the Congress of Vienna, although Talleyrand somewhat deprecatingly referred to the 'quantities enumerated by political arithmeticians' (above, p. 100). A noteworthy feature of this chart is the analysis of the rise and fall of the major powers which is given in the remarks.

Statistical Chart of Europe (1804)

States	Great Britain	France	Russia	Turkey	Prussia	Sweden
North, South, and middle of Europe	M.	M.	N.	S.	N.	N.
Extent in Square Miles	106,000	150,000	4,650,000	780,600	50,000	209,000
Number of Inhabitants	14,000,000	26,000,000	25,000,000	24,000,000	5,600,000	3,000,000
Acres	67,000,000	95,600,000	3,000,000,000	510,000,000	34,000,000	133,000,000
Acres in cultivation	40,000,000	76,000,000	160,000,000	128,000,000	25,000,000	24,000,000
Acres to each Person	$4\frac{3}{4}$	$3\frac{1}{2}$	120	21	6	44
Debt	400,000,000	260,000,000	10,000,000	None	None	7,000,000
Revenues	27,000,000	19,000,000	7,600,000	7,000,000	4,200,000	1,560,000
Average Exports to England annually (to all parts)	30,000,000	45,000	1,500,000	270,000	213,600	290,000
Imports from England annually (to all parts)	25,000,000	160,000	560,000	280,000	115,000	170,000
Soldiers in time of Peace	46,000	230,000	380,000	250,000	225,000	50,000
Soldiers in time of War	400,000	600,000	560,000	380,060	360,000	140,000
Sailors in Peace	18,000	25,000	20,000	32,000	13,000	16,000
Sailors in War	114,000	125,000	40,000	56,000	30,000	36,000
Ships, Frigates, &c.	958	266	130	190	86	103
Taxes on each Person	£2	15s.	7s.	7s.	14s.	10s.

Denmark	Germany	Emperors own Dominions	Poland before its dis- memberment	Spain	Portugal	Holland
N.	M.	M.	N.	S.	S.	M.
170,600	196,600	180,500	162,000	148,000	27,000	10,000
2,155,000	25,100,000	20,000,000	18,000,000	12,000,000	1,840,000	2,760,000
10,000,000	126,000,000	116,000,000	105,000,000	95,000,000	17,280,000	6,400,000
12,700,000	93,000,000	75,000,000	40,000,000	40,000,000	9,000,000	4,600,000
54	5	6	6	8	10	2½
2,700,000	45,000,000	41,000,000	31,000,000	47,000,000	4,000,000	12,000,000
1,530,000	14,000,000	11,600,000	610,000	14,000,000	2,160,000	3,600,000
108,600	960,000	390,000	167,000	605,000	500,000	650,000
210,000	1,400,000	1,800,000	206,000	1,500,000	900,000	1,800,000
76,000	120,000	260,000	20,000	105,000	36,000	36,000
210,000	250,000	460,000	100,000	250,000	60,000	70,000
18,000	None	None	None	40,000	12,000	17,000
29,000	None	None	None	105,000	23,000	41,000
97	None	None	None	128	61	90
15s.	11s.	12s.	1s. 6d.	£1 5s.	£1 3s.	£1 12s.

Statistical Chart of Europe (1804)

The utility of this Chart is too obvious to need explanation.—At one view, is presented to the eye, such a statement of every Country in Europe, that will enable us to form a better idea thereof, than any book ever published; for in a few hours you may obtain more compleat knowledge than could possibly be procured in many months: for here the mind is deeply impressed even at firstsight.—Instead of seeking for this information by turning over innumerable pages of various authors, which renders the pursuit expensive, tedious, and difficult; it is here presented to the eye, easy, cheap, and familiar.

REMARKS—GREAT BRITAIN.—By its admirable laws, not only still preserves its rank and dignity as a first rate power, but rears its venerable and majestic head above the ruins of surrounding states; and whilst some have fell, and others on the eve of falling, by tamely trembling at the foes advance; Britain alone has dared to scorn their frowns, and smiles contemptuously on the adventurous Chief.[1]—RUSSIA.—Including its Asiatic Domains, is considerably larger than all Europe together.—About 200 years since, it was one of the most inconsiderable states existing; since which period, it has greatly increased in power and territory. Peter the Great united Siberia to this empire. The eminent virtues and valour of this Prince contributed amazingly to the prosperity of his people. —PRUSSIA—is also a first rate power, and that very deservingly; the wisdom and valour of its rulers hath raised it from obscurity, only so late as about 100 years back, to its present florishing state; and while other nations are involved in debt, Prussia has none to pay; and still rich and powerful: courted by its neighbours, and feared by its enemies; it may one day become a second Rome.—TURKEY.—Although next to Russia in extent of territory, seems on the decline, its powerful neighbours may ere long bring it to the fate of other nations. All human institutions have their end; while small ones rise, the great ones often fall.—GERMANY.—Like many other States seems too much within the grasp of France, but well for this empire it has at its head a Prince,[2] who in his own hereditary possessions, is more powerful than all the rest of the Princes of the empire together; and happy are they if they know their happiness consists in a strict union with the house of Austria, that Gallic power may not make irreparable havock among them.— SWEDEN.—By its good policy, preserves its rank as a second rate power.—DENMARK,—was formerly higher in the rank of nations than at present, but still preserves its dignity as a second power.—SPAIN.—Has fell from the first of nations to a second class, and almost beneath even that, so much for gold, luxury, and idleness.—PORTUGAL.—Like Spain, has lost its ancient splendour; their emigration for the pursuit of gold, and neglect of agriculture, manufacture, &c. hath almost thrown it out of the scale of nations.—HOLLAND.—Once the most industrious and florishing state in Europe, has now become a mere province of France.—POLAND.—From a first rate power, has at length been annihilated, and fell to the joint shares of Prussia, Austria, and Russia. Cast your eye above to the revenues of Poland, and who can wonder it is no more a nation; although extensive, populous, and a brave and warlike people, they had not the means to support their dignity.— FRANCE.—By the force of arms, has gained the ascendency of continental power. Many happy and florishing states are now beneath their galling yoke; and fortunate indeed will others be, if (not too late), by unanimity, they are enabled like Britain, to bid defiance to its power.

[1] Napoleon.
[2] Francis II, the last Holy Roman Emperor, who had to be content with being Francis I, Emperor of Austria, after Napoleon assumed the imperial title in 1806.

Index

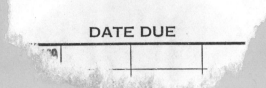